# Make Your Own
# DINOSAUR
## out of Chicken Bones

◆◆◆◆◆◆◆◆◆◆◆◆

# MAKE YOUR OWN

# DINOSAUR

## OUT OF CHICKEN BONES

••••••••••••

## FOOLPROOF INSTRUCTIONS
## FOR BUDDING PALEONTOLOGISTS

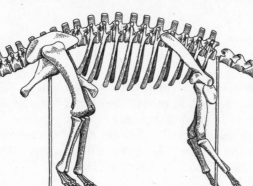

# CHRIS MCGOWAN
## ILLUSTRATED BY JULIAN MULOCK

HarperPerennial
A Division of HarperCollinsPublishers

HarperCollins books may be purchased for educational, business, or sales promotional use. For information please write: Special Markets Department, HarperCollins Publishers, Inc., 10 East 53rd Street, New York, NY 10022.

FIRST EDITION

Designed by Nancy Singer

ISBN 0-06-095226-1

99 00 01 ❖/RRD 10 9 8 7

TO JILL, WHO TOOK THE
DINOSAUR OUT OF THE CLOSET

# CONTENTS

••••••••••••

# ACKNOWLEDGMENTS

◆◆◆◆◆◆◆◆◆◆◆

This book is very different from anything else I have ever written. In these cautious days of fiscal restraint, it took an enterprising publisher to make it happen, and I thank the good people at HarperCollins for this. I thank them for their spirit of adventure, for their unrestrained enthusiasm, and for their sense of fun—it has been a great pleasure working with such professionals. In particular I want to thank my editors: Jennifer Griffin, who acquired the manuscript, and Sharon Bowers, who took up the flag and was always available with help, encouragement, and advice. My thanks also to Jane Hardick and Dina Post, who produced the book; Nancy Singer, who designed it; Keonaona Peterson, for copyediting; Debbie Gazaway, for proofreading; Renato Stanisic, for designing the cover; and David Hughes, who took the photograph. HarperCollins spared no effort in promoting the book, and I thank Elaine Brosnan and Craig Herman for their zealous and imaginative pursuit of publicity.

HarperCollins would never have considered publishing this book had it not been introduced to them by my agent, Jill Grinberg, of Scovil, Chichak and Galen. My writing career changed from night into day when Jill began representing me. No words can express my sincere gratitude and thanks.

It was with much trepidation that I showed copies of this unorthodox manuscript to my paleontological colleagues for their criticisms. Their opinions mean a great deal to me, but what on earth would they think of my efforts this time? Phil Currie, Nicholas Hotton, and John McIntosh generously agreed to read the manuscript. To my profound relief, each one was very positive, giving confidence and encouragement when it was most needed. I thank them for this boost and for their valuable comments. My thanks also to Olivier Rieppel, with whom I discussed the manuscript and who also gave enthusiastic encouragement and help.

Some time ago, my good friend and illustrator, Julian Mulock, paid me a visit, following my cryptic invitation. While beating about the subject of a new project, I leaned behind the sofa and produced Basil, the prototype dinosaur. Julian was suitably impressed and has been an active participant in the project ever since. Working with Julian has been the same mixture of dedication and fun as it always is, for which I thank him.

Andy Forester, raconteur, cordon bleu, and lifelong friend, shared his recipe for garlic soup that I hope I have faithfully reproduced. Thanks, Andy.

I am remarkably fortunate to work at a museum that still values the importance of research and scholarship. I am also fortunate to have a cross-appointment to the Department of Zoology of the University of Toronto. I have the best of both worlds—collections to stimulate the curiosity and students to challenge my interpretations of them. I wish to thank both institutions for their support over the years, enabling me to pursue my interests in the worlds of both the living and the extinct.

The Natural Sciences and Engineering Research Council of Canada has funded my research for two decades, for which I express my thanks and gratitude.

My last thanks is to my long-suffering wife, Liz—she who endures chicken carcasses, messy kitchens, and lost times as I work away in my room; she who patiently proofreads my work when she has so much of her own to do; she who encourages, supports, and nurtures. What would be the point if it weren't for you?

# PART 1

# DINOSAURS ARE ALIVE AND WELL

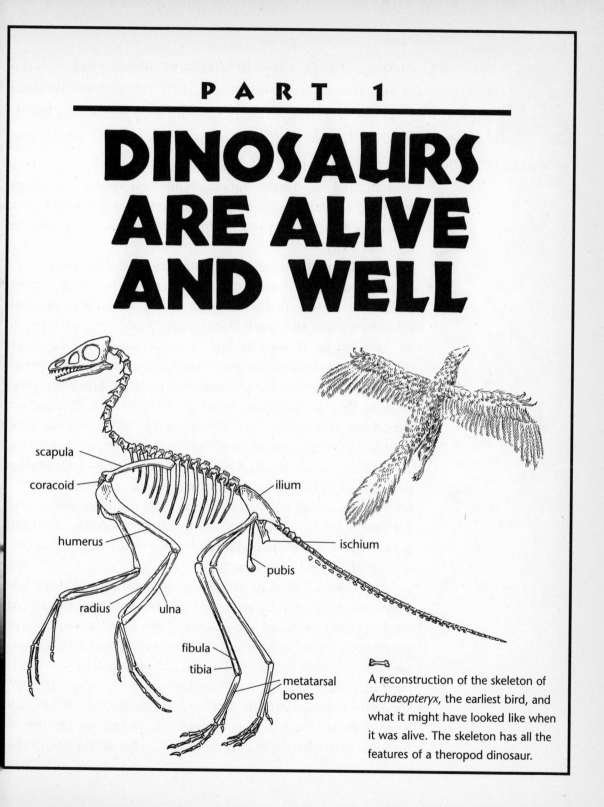

A reconstruction of the skeleton of *Archaeopteryx*, the earliest bird, and what it might have looked like when it was alive. The skeleton has all the features of a theropod dinosaur.

**A** few years ago, one of the guards at the museum where I work reported that she had just discovered a distraught little boy in our dinosaur gallery. "He was sobbing his eyes out," she told me. "Absolutely heart-broken. And when I asked him why he was so upset, he said it was because all the dinosaurs were dead."

I hurried out to the gallery, hoping to console him, but when I got there, he was gone. If I had found him, I would have explained that the dinosaurs were not really dead: They live on today as birds.

The idea that birds evolved from dinosaurs dates back more than a century, and was inspired by the discovery of a most remarkable fossil called *Archaeopteryx.* This 180-million-year-old creature, the size of a small chicken, was found to be reptilian in all its features—it was, in fact, a small dinosaur. Like other dinosaurs of its kind, collectively called **theropods**, it was **bipedal** (walking on two legs) and possessed all the other dinosaurian features of its close relatives. What made this small dinosaur so remarkable was that it had feathers. Its feathered forelimbs were modified as wings, and its long, bony tail was fringed with feathers. In life, the tail would have looked something like that of a magpie. But in modern birds, the tail is formed entirely of feathers that are considerably longer than those of *Archaeopteryx,* and are attached at their base to a stubby appendage, often called the parson's nose. The small bones inside the parson's nose are all that remain of the bird's tail skeleton.

*Archaeopteryx,* with its mixture of dinosaurian and avian features, was discovered in 1860, just one year after publication of Darwin's controversial *On the Origin of Species.* Charles Darwin's proponents seized upon this link between reptiles and birds as tangible evidence for evolution—the theory that living organisms had evolved from earlier forms, rather than having been specially created as described in the Bible in the book of Genesis. Thomas Henry Huxley, one of Darwin's most zealous supporters, made an extensive study of *Archaeopteryx,* comparing it with the

# Theropods and Other Dinosaur Groups

The theropods are a large group of dinosaurs that includes *Tyrannosaurus, Allosaurus, Velociraptor, Ornithomimus, Oviraptor, Coelophysis,* and, of course, *Archaeopteryx* and all other birds. The theropods share a number of specialized features, including a hand with three fingers,[1] all ending in claws; a foot supported by three long **metatarsal** bones, which are tightly pressed together and are often fused (joined); three main toes and a short big toe, all ending in claws; a **femur** (thighbone) that is slightly bowed forward; a **fibula** (the thin bone that runs along the outside of the shinbone) that is closely pressed against the **tibia** (shinbone); and thin-walled, hollow limb bones.

Theropods, like their sister group the **sauropods,** to which *Apatosaurus* belongs, have a three-pronged pelvis, comprising the **ilium** (above), the **pubis** (in front), and the **ischium** (behind). Many theropods, including birds, have a long ilium that extends well forward of the hip socket. Sauropods, in contrast, have a much shorter and broader ilium. Dinosaurs with a three-pronged pelvis are collectively referred to as the **Saurischia.** All other dinosaurs have a four-pronged pelvis and are collectively called the **Ornithischia.** Ornithischian dinosaurs include the hadrosaurs, stegosaurs, horned dinosaurs, and ankylosaurs.

---

[1] Some theropods, including *Tyrannosaurus,* have only two fingers.

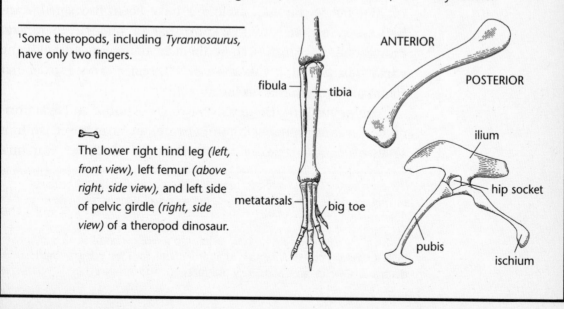

The lower right hind leg *(left, front view),* left femur *(above right, side view),* and left side of pelvic girdle *(right, side view)* of a theropod dinosaur.

fibula — tibia

metatarsals — big toe

ANTERIOR

POSTERIOR

ilium

hip socket

pubis

ischium

few dinosaurs that were known at that time. His painstaking comparisons showed that *Archaeopteryx* was a dinosaur in all its skeletal features. As has often been said, it would have been identified as a dinosaur had it not been for the preservation of feather impressions. Indeed, one of the five other *Archaeopteryx* skeletons that have since been found was classified as a dinosaur for many years because its faint feather impressions had gone unnoticed. Huxley's study of *Archaeopteryx*, the earliest and most primitive bird,[2] convinced him that birds had evolved from dinosaurs. This hypothesis was widely accepted and persisted well into the present century. However, it was rejected in 1926, following the publication of Gerhard Heilman's influential study on avian ancestry, *The Origin of Birds*. Heilman recognized that *Archaeopteryx* had much in common with small theropod dinosaurs, but a single anatomical feature disqualified dinosaurs from being its ancestor. The feature in question was the paired clavicles, or collarbones, which form part of the shoulder girdle. *Archaeopteryx*, like most modern birds, has a wishbone, or **furcula**, believed to represent the fused clavicles. However, Heilman pointed out that theropods had lost their clavicles, so they were already too specialized to have given rise to birds.

Many new dinosaur skeletons have been discovered since Heilman's time, and we now know that a number of theropods actually have a furcula. These include *Allosaurus*, *Albertosaurus* (close relative of *Tyrannosaurus*), *Oviraptor*, and *Ingenia*, so Heilman's objection is no longer valid.[3]

The revival of Huxley's thesis that birds evolved from dinosaurs is attributable to John Ostrom, of Yale University. In a series of eloquent papers published in the 1970s, he convinc-

---

[2] An even earlier fossil, *Protoavis*, has been described from the Late Triassic (*Archaeopteryx* is Late Jurassic in age), but its avian identity has been widely questioned.

[3] Incidentally, *Oviraptor* and *Ingenia* belong to a rare group of small and lightly built dinosaurs, called oviraptors, that are unique for their peculiar short, deep skulls, which are completely toothless.

ingly demonstrated the close similarities between *Archaeopteryx* and small theropod dinosaurs. The fact that some theropods had retained the furcula, while some modern birds (parrots) had lost it, removed any lingering doubts that theropods were ancestral to birds, yet a few paleontologists remained unconvinced. However, so much additional evidence has accumulated during the last two decades of dinosaurian discoveries that almost all paleontologists are now agreed that birds evolved from dinosaurs. Indeed, since birds are now classified as theropods, it is perfectly correct to refer to birds as dinosaurs. I certainly have no problems with this, and, as recent discoveries have shown— like the feathered dinosaurs from China (named *Sinosauropteryx prima*) and the dinosaurlike birds from Madagascar—the distinction between birds and dinosaurs has become indistinct. However, unlike many of my colleagues, I still think it useful to retain the terms *birds* and *dinosaurs,* rather than using the terms *avian dinosaurs* and *nonavian dinosaurs*. I will therefore continue to use the words *dinosaur* and *bird* below, according to common usage, cognizant that birds really are dinosaurs.

Given that birds are dinosaurs, why does the skeleton of, say, a chicken, look so different from that of *Tyrannosaurus*? The reason mostly has to do with what happens during the later stages of a bird's development. If you looked at the skeleton of a developing bird embryo you would see a great deal of similarity with a theropod dinosaur. But, as development proceeds, many of the bones that were separate become fused together, losing their individual identity. Therefore, by the time the bird hatches, or at least before it reaches maturity, it has lost most of its similarities with its dinosaurian ancestors. The following examples will illustrate the point.

Theropods have three fingers, the middle one of which is the longest. Birds have a similar hand structure during the early stages of their development. However, as the embryo continues growing inside the shell, the first finger (the thumb) begins to lag behind the others. It eventually becomes so small compared

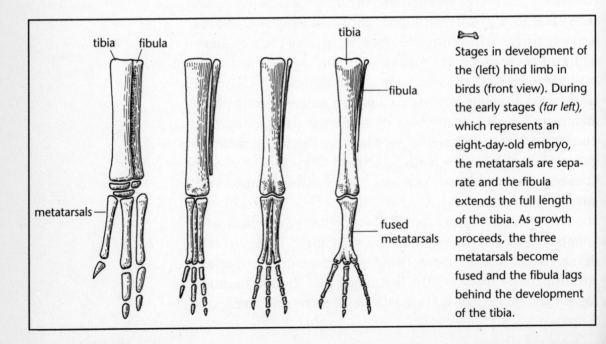

Stages in the development of the (left) hand in birds. The three-fingered stage at the far left was drawn from an eight-day-old duck embryo, while the fused-up stage at the far right represents the adult condition.

radius ulna

thumb (1)

second finger (2)

third finger (3)

1

2

3

1

2

3

1

2

3

to the others that it almost disappears. The third finger also grows more slowly than the middle finger, and eventually fuses with it. As a result of these changes, the hand of an adult bird looks nothing like that of the average dinosaur.

tibia fibula

metatarsals

tibia

fibula

fused metatarsals

Stages in development of the (left) hind limb in birds (front view). During the early stages *(far left)*, which represents an eight-day-old embryo, the metatarsals are separate and the fibula extends the full length of the tibia. As growth proceeds, the three metatarsals become fused and the fibula lags behind the development of the tibia.

## Why the Bird's Tibia Outgrows the Fibula

◆◆◆◆◆◆◆◆◆◆◆◆◆◆◆◆◆◆◆◆◆◆◆◆◆◆◆◆◆◆◆◆◆◆◆◆◆◆◆◆◆◆◆◆◆◆◆◆◆◆◆◆

It seems that the tibia grows more rapidly than the fibula because it outcompetes the fibula for nutrients. This has been shown experimentally by inserting a small partition between the developing fibula and tibia. Under these conditions the growing fibula gets all the nutrients it needs, and increases in length at the same rate as the tibia.

Theropods have three long metatarsal bones in the lower leg, in the part that is equivalent to the sole of our foot. Birds are no exception to this, and have three long and separate metatarsal bones during the early stages of their development. However, as growth continues, the three bones move closer together, and eventually fuse. The process is not completed until sometime after hatching, so the sutures (joins) between the three bones can usually be seen in chicks, and in some other young birds. As the bird reaches maturity the sutures disappear completely, and the only indication that the single bone once comprised three parts is shown by the three **condyles** (knuckles) at the end. Each of these condyles articulates (forms a joint) with one of the three toes.

Theropods, like other **tetrapods** (four-limbed animals), have two bones in their lower leg. The outer one, the fibula, is only about half as thick as the tibia (or less), but is the same length. Birds retain this feature during early development, but the growth of the tibia soon overtakes that of the fibula. Consequently, by the time the bird reaches maturity, its fibula has become reduced to a slender splint of bone which is only about half as long as the tibia.

Although birds lose many of their theropod features during development, other features are retained. These include a curved femur; closely placed fibula and tibia; a foot with three main toes and a short big toe, all of which end in claws; thin-walled, hollow limb bones; and a long ilium that extends well forward of the hip socket. Birds also retain much of the theropod shape of their **humerus** (upper arm bone) and of their vertebrae. Therefore, it is possible to build a model dinosaur skeleton from a bird's skeleton by modifying its bones.

Millions of chickens are consumed every day, so there is no shortage of chicken bones from which to build dinosaur models. Unfortunately, modern processing practices discard the chicken's lower legs, feet, and head, but these deficiencies can be overcome. When you work your way through the next section, you will end up with a realistic model of that quintessential dinosaur *Apatosaurus,* also known—incorrectly—as *Brontosaurus.* I will not pretend that this can be accomplished in an afternoon—my first *Apatosaurus* took seventeen hours to build—but it is not difficult, and you will learn something about birds and dinosaurs along the way. And since birds really are dinosaurs, the result will be a *real* dinosaur skeleton.

# PART 2

# HOW TO BUILD AN APATOSAURUS SKELETON

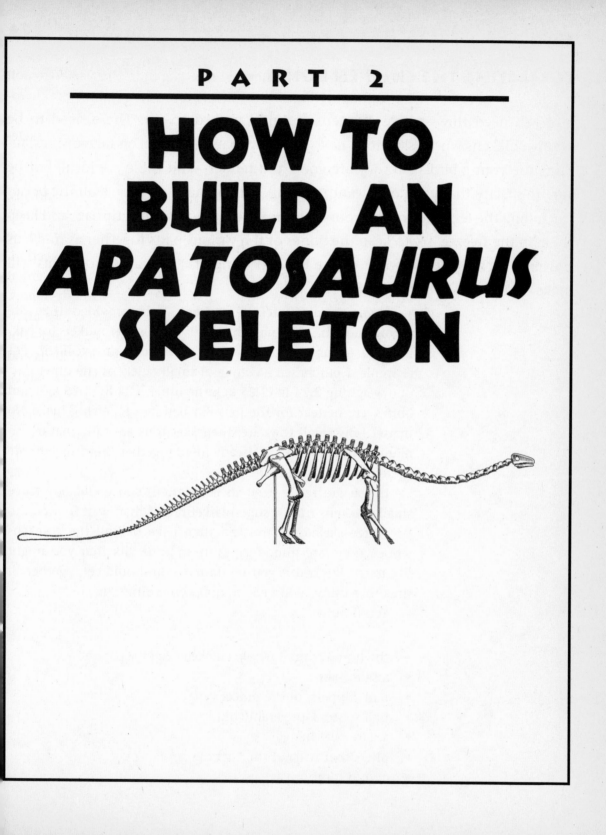

## COLLECTING THE CHICKEN BONES

You will need three whole chickens to build your dinosaur. These need to be young chickens whose skeletons have not fully matured. Chicken take-out restaurants use young birds—so they are good and tender—and these are ideal, but be sure to specify that you don't want it cut up. All you need do is save all the bones (including the legs and wings) from your meal, seal them in a plastic bag, and keep them in the freezer. Try to keep the bones of the various parts together as much as possible (such as all the bones of the left leg) using plastic wrap or foil. This will make it much easier for you later on.

Home-cooked chickens are fine, too, provided they are young enough. The small chickens sold in supermarkets for baking and frying are young birds, and these are excellent. For example, I purchased a couple of small chickens the other day, one weighing 2.74 lb (1.25 kg), the other 3.84 lb (1.75 kg), and both were perfect for the job. But beware of stewing hens! No matter how small they are, their skeletons are fully mature, so many of their bones are already fused together. Stewing hens are therefore to be avoided.

If you are really keen to get started, you could buy three small chickens from a supermarket rather than wait to accumulate three skeletons. You can then bake or boil the chickens whole; there are some recipes in an appendix that you might like to try. But before getting started, you should get together all the other things you need to build your dinosaur.

You'll need:

- the bones from 3 whole chickens, kept separate
- a saucepan
- nail clippers, of the pincer type
- nail scissors, preferably old
- a wire coat hanger
- pliers that will cut the coat hanger
- an old toothbrush

- a plastic mesh scouring pad
- a table knife
- a teaspoon
- a dinner plate
- a nail file or emery board
- floral tape (green wax tape, from craft shop or florist)
- a pipe cleaner (6 inches or 15 cm long)
- roll of plastic twist ties (from craft shop or garden supplier)
- plastic sandwich bags
- paper towels
- toothpicks
- cotton swabs, such as Q-Tips
- masking tape
- four small paper clips
- tube of clear glue or cement, such as Uhu
- Spackle, Polyfilla, or plaster of paris
- white Plasticine
- a dishrag
- an X-Acto knife or scalpel
- a piece of wood, approximately 2 feet long by 5 inches wide and ¾-inch deep (60 cm x 10 cm x 2.0 cm)—this is for the base of the stand. A piece of wooden molding from a lumberyard works well; some shops supply pieces of finished wood as "craft board."
- 10 paper plates
- a few paper cups
- a pencil and some index cards for making labels
- a ruler, with metric and English units
- a small plastic garbage or grocery bag


Optional extras:

- Krazy Glue
- safety glasses
- a 60-watt table lamp, preferably with a metal shade

- fine forceps or tweezers
- dividers, or a compass
- an electric drill
- long-nosed pliers
- two empty tuna or other shallow tins
- two cupfuls of sand
- liquid laundry bleach

The measurements used in this book are in imperial (British) units and metric units. Scientists always employ metric units, which are much easier to use, and in some parts of the book, where precise measurements are required, only metric units are given. As in the first part of the book, when proper terms are used for the first time they are printed in bold. Anatomical directions will be used for orientations, namely: **anterior** (front), **posterior** (back), **dorsal** (top), **ventral** (bottom), **lateral** (outside), and **medial** (inside). Krazy Glue is a useful option for some of the gluing jobs, but clear glue, which is more user friendly, can be used throughout. Youngsters should certainly not use Krazy Glue.

## BOILING THE BONES

**Warning: Youngsters should not do this without an adult helper.**

It is easiest to boil and process one chicken at a time, at least to start with. Once you've completed one chicken, you might want to try processing the other two at the same time. If you decide to do this, boil them up in separate saucepans, so that the bones do not become mixed. All chicken carcasses need boiling, even if they have been previously cooked. If you are starting with an uncooked chicken and decide to boil it rather than bake it (boiling gives best results), follow the procedure as set out below. This will yield chicken stock for making Andy Forester's Famous Garlic Soup, as well as meat for some other meals. Recipes are given in an appendix.

## PROCESSING PREVIOUSLY COOKED CHICKENS

Put the chicken carcass into a saucepan, cover with water, and boil it for one to one-and-a-half hours. Do not overboil, or else the bones may become too brittle. If your chicken was baked in the oven, only boil it for an hour. Once boiled, remove the saucepan from the stove, put it in the sink, and gently flush with cold water until the contents are cold enough to handle.

## PROCESSING UNCOOKED CHICKENS

If you are going to roast or fry the chicken, collect all the parts up after the meal and process as above. Incidentally, you might like to follow McGowan's recipe for honey-roasted chicken, given in the recipe appendix.

If you are going to boil the chicken, proceed as follows. Remove the neck, gizzard, and liver from the body cavity and place them in a saucepan with the bird. Add enough water to cover the bird, close the lid, and bring to a boil. Turn down the heat and simmer for one-and-a-half hours.

Using a fish slice or spatula and large spoon, carefully transfer the chicken and the neck segment to a bowl. Replace the lid on the saucepan and bring the stock back to a boil. Run cold tap water into the bowl, allowing time for the chicken to cool down. Separate and clean the bones, as outlined below, but start with the wings and legs. Save the meat in a plastic freezer bag, refrigerating for later use (see recipe appendix). Return all other soft parts and unwanted bones to the saucepan as they are removed.

Allow the stock to simmer for at least an hour, then strain off into a bowl. Cover the bowl (to exclude bacteria) while the chicken stock cools to room temperature, then transfer to the refrigerator. Once chilled, the solidified fat is easily removed from the top. Transfer the gelatinous stock to a freezer bag, seal and label it, and store it in the freezer until needed.

## SEPARATING AND CLEANING THE BONES

This step involves separating the bones, removing the meat, washing them, and leaving them to dry.

Be gentle when handling the bones, because many of them are fragile and easily broken. As each bone is removed, clean it by rinsing with water. Remove any remaining scraps of meat by gently scrubbing with the toothbrush. Pieces of cartilage (gristle) can be removed from the ends of the long bones (of the legs and wings) by scrubbing with the plastic scouring pad. As is true of all vertebrates, most of a chicken's skeleton is formed of cartilage during the early stages of development. As development proceeds, the cartilage becomes **ossified**, that is, it is replaced by bone. The ends of bones are the last to ossify, hence the caps of cartilage at the ends of the long bones.

You'll need to identify the bones as they are removed, but don't worry, you'll be told how to do this! Once you've identified a bone, label it so you can name it later on.

Sometimes you will be told to note whether the bone is from the left or right side.

To make a label, cut a piece of card about an inch (3 cm) square, and write the information in pencil. Writing in pencil is the easiest way of making a permanent record and has been used for many years for labeling pickled specimens in museums. Ink, on the other hand, runs, and soon becomes illegible. Make a small hole in the label with the point of your scissors and attach it to the bone with a length of plastic twist tie. Sometimes a label will be placed beside a group of similar bones, or enclosed inside a plastic bag of bones, instead of labeling each separately. Leave the cleaned and labeled bones to dry on paper plates lined with paper towels. The scraps of meat and gristle, together with unwanted bones, can be added to the stock in the saucepan or disposed of in the garbage bag.

## STEP 1: SEPARATING AND CLEANING THE BONES OF THE BOILED CARCASS

Note: If this is a previously uncooked chicken, begin by removing the wings and legs.

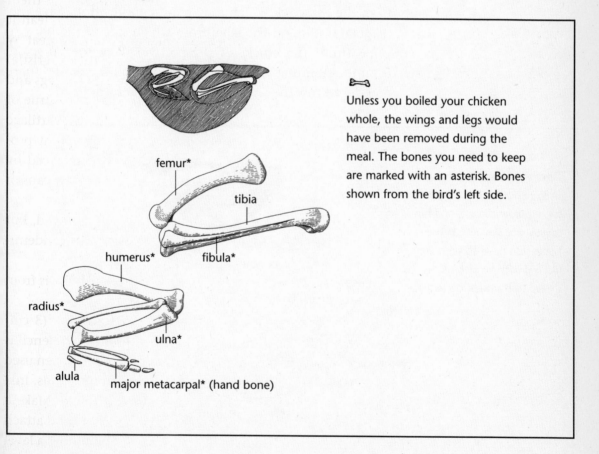

Unless you boiled your chicken whole, the wings and legs would have been removed during the meal. The bones you need to keep are marked with an asterisk. Bones shown from the bird's left side.

femur*

tibia

humerus*

fibula*

radius*

ulna*

alula

major metacarpal* (hand bone)

1. Lay the remains of the chicken on the dinner plate and locate the breast region.

2. Using your fingers, remove the loose meat from the side of the rib cage to uncover the shoulder. The **pectoral girdle** (shoulder) is in two parts. The upper part, the **scapula** (shoulder blade), is long and slender and is attached to the ribs by muscles. The lower part, the **coracoid**, is thicker and shorter, and is firmly attached to the front of the **sternum** (breastbone). Birds, unlike most other tetrapods, have the pectoral girdle rigidly attached to the rest of the skeleton. This is to give a firm anchorage for the flapping wings.

   Lift the scapula so that it just comes free from the rib cage—it will come away very easily. Separate the scapula from the coracoid, which may require more effort. Save the scapula, noting on the label from which side of the body it came (from the chicken's perspective). Free the coracoid from the sternum—you may have to pull a little harder than you did to free the scapula. Discard the coracoid.

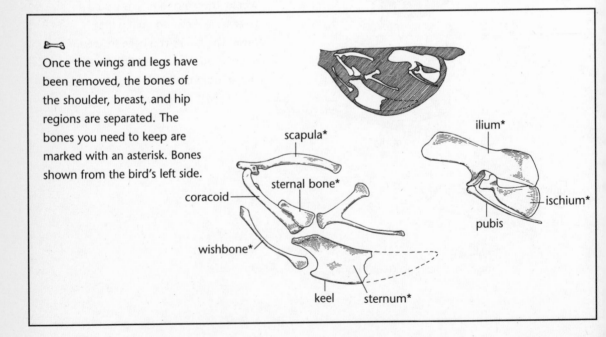

Once the wings and legs have been removed, the bones of the shoulder, breast, and hip regions are separated. The bones you need to keep are marked with an asterisk. Bones shown from the bird's left side.

scapula*

coracoid

sternal bone*

wishbone*

keel    sternum*

ilium*

ischium*

pubis

3. Repeat step 2 for the other side of the chicken.

4. Remove the sternum, which is attached to the rib cage, and save it (it will be used for making the skull). Notice the large vertical flange, the **keel**. Most birds, including the chicken, are fliers, and their deeply keeled sternum provides a large attachment area for the muscles that power the wings. Look for a spade-shaped bone (about 1 inch or 2.5 cm long) attached to the anterior dorsal region (front top corner) of the sternum. There is one on either side. We'll call these the **sternal bones**. They are part of the developing sternum, and will eventually fuse with the main part of that bone as the bird matures. The sternal bones will be used for part of the dinosaur's coracoid. Look for the wishbone (furcula). We'll use this for part of the dinosaur's tail.

5. Remove the ribs from one side of the vertebral column, recording from which side each rib came. You'll probably find six ribs on either side, each with a forked end where it articulates with its corresponding vertebra. Some of the ribs are attached at their lower end to a second bone, which

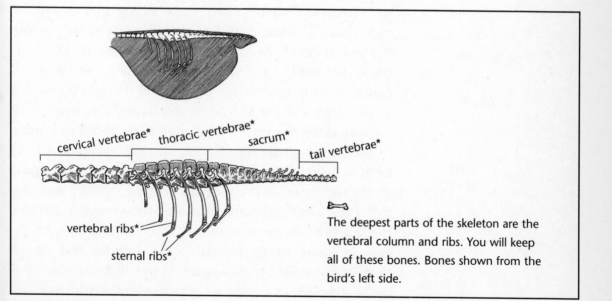

cervical vertebrae*    thoracic vertebrae*    sacrum*    tail vertebrae*

vertebral ribs*

sternal ribs*

The deepest parts of the skeleton are the vertebral column and ribs. You will keep all of these bones. Bones shown from the bird's left side.

attaches to the sternum. These bones are called **sternal ribs**, to distinguish them from the **vertebral ribs** (true ribs). There are five pairs of sternal ribs. Some of the sternal ribs will be used for making the feet, others for making part of the tail. Save all the ribs, separating them into two groups—labeled *vertebral ribs* (forked) and *sternal ribs*. The vertebral ribs are also divided into two sets, labeled *right ribs* and *left ribs*. Place the ribs on their own paper plate, with the labels.

As you clean each rib, you will notice a small cartilaginous process, about halfway down on the posterior edge. As a chicken matures, this will **ossify**, forming the **uncinate process**. The uncinate process of one rib overlaps the rib behind it, increasing the rigidity of the rib cage. This is a flight modification of the skeleton to make it more rigid.

Humans also have sternal ribs, but they remain cartilaginous. Ossification of the sternal ribs in birds is yet another modification for making their skeleton more rigid.

6. Repeat step 5 for the other side.
7. Straighten an 8-inch (20 cm) length of plastic twist tie. Starting at the neck end, thread this through the centers of the vertebrae. This is to keep them all together and in the right order. The idea is to feed the plastic twist tie through the **neural canal** of each vertebra, the channel that conveys the **spinal cord.** You will probably be able to see the spinal cord as a fairly thick white thread, and this will give you a target to aim for. You should be able to push the twist tie all the way along the vertebral column, as far as the beginning of the **pelvic girdle** (pelvis). Remove the meat and sinews from the vertebral column and see where it joins the pelvic girdle. Gently break the vertebral column at this point. You may have some difficulty separating the vertebrae, because the last two—those immediately anterior to the pelvic girdle—are quite firmly united to the anterior end of the **sacrum**, the series of fused vertebrae to which the pelvic girdle is attached. Once you have separated the vertebral col-

umn, you should be able to thread the twist tie all the way through. If there are still one or two vertebrae attaching to the anterior end of the pelvic girdle, gently try to break them free. Add them to the twist tie, without changing their orientation. Join the two ends of the twist tie to secure the vertebrae. If you were unable to thread the twist tie through the vertebral column, just remove the vertebrae one at a time, starting with the neck end, removing the meat as you go. As each vertebra comes free, thread it onto the twist tie. Whichever method you use, you should finish up with about 12 or 13 vertebrae on the twist tie.

The individual vertebrae can now be separated from one another and scrubbed clean of meat and cartilage, using the toothbrush. When clean, label this string *neck and back vertebrae*. Attach the label to the neck end, so as to record which way around they go. (If you forget, there's an easy way of checking—see *How the Vertebrae Fit Together* on page 32.)

If you used a take-out chicken, you will have all the available **cervical** (neck) vertebrae on the twist tie. However, if you cooked it yourself, you will probably have a separate neck section (the piece that gets put inside the chicken's body cavity). In this case, take a second length of twist tie, and thread it through the neck vertebrae. Join the two ends of the twist tie, clean the individual vertebrae as before, and label them *anterior neck vertebrae*. Attach this short string to the neck end of the string of vertebrae labeled *neck and back vertebrae*. Put onto a paper plate labeled *vertebrae*.

8. Find the pelvic girdle. Look at the left side first. If the leg is still attached, take it off and keep it for later. The pelvic girdle is in two halves, right and left, and each half is made up of three separate bones. The upper bone, the ilium, is about 3 inches long (7 cm). It is attached medially (on the inside) to part of the vertebral column. It is also attached to the two other bones that make up the pelvic girdle—the ischium, which is triangular, and the pubis, which is long and slender.

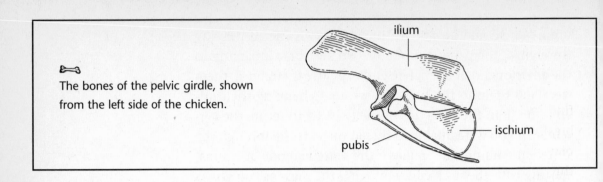

The bones of the pelvic girdle, shown from the left side of the chicken.

ilium

pubis

ischium

Using your fingers, clear away the cartilage, thereby separating the ilium from the underlying vertebrae, and the ischium from the ilium and pubis. Save the ilium and ischium, labeling each one, but discard the pubis. It is important to note to which side they belong.

9. Repeat step 8 for the right side of the pelvis.
10. Look at what is left of the vertebral column. The first part, the sacrum (strictly called the synsacrum), is about 2 inches (5 cm) long, and is where the ilium was attached. You'll be able to count up to 11 or 12 vertebrae, and these are firmly joined together, making the sacrum rigid. A moveable fleshy pad, sometimes called the parson's nose, is attached to the

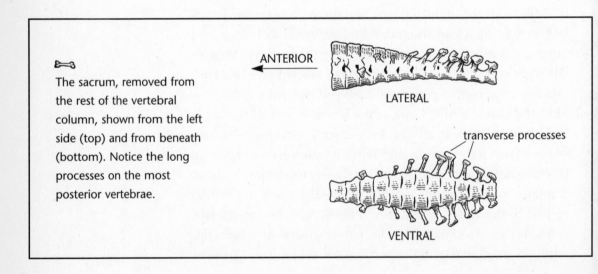

The sacrum, removed from the rest of the vertebral column, shown from the left side (top) and from beneath (bottom). Notice the long processes on the most posterior vertebrae.

ANTERIOR

LATERAL

transverse processes

VENTRAL

end of the sacrum. This is the chicken's tail; it contains several small vertebrae.

11. Remove the parson's nose, making sure not to lose any of the tail vertebrae. Squeeze it between your finger and thumb to find the vertebrae inside. It is very soft and fatty and easily breaks up. Remove the fatty material and save all the vertebrae. Birds regularly preen their feathers, running them through their bills to keep them clean and oiled. They obtain the oil from the base of the parson's nose. Separate the tail vertebrae and put them onto the paper plate labeled *vertebrae*. Draw a circle around them and label this *tail vertebrae*.

12. Boil the sacrum in a small saucepan for 10–15 minutes. This is to soften the joints between the individual vertebrae, making them easier to separate. Remove the sacrum from the saucepan and allow it to cool. Look at it. You'll see that the vertebrae at the posterior end have large **transverse processes**, the bony protrusions that extend from either side of each vertebra. They confirm which way the sacrum faces. There should be 11 or 12 vertebrae. Using a knife, strip off the plastic covering from a 10-inch (25 cm) length of twist tie, freeing the wire. Thread the wire through the neural canals of the vertebrae, as you did for the other vertebrae, twisting the two ends together to form a loop. Carefully clear away any remaining soft parts with the toothbrush.

Using gentle finger pressure, try separating the two vertebrae at either end of the sacrum, taking care not to break off any bony processes. They will probably come free all right, and you may be able to remove one or two others, but the rest will probably have to be cut apart. Lay the sacrum down on a damp dishrag, ventral surface up, so that the **neural spines**, the bony processes that project from the top of the vertebrae, face away from you. Notice the obvious suture lines between adjacent vertebrae. Starting at the anterior end of the sacrum, place the blade point of an X-Acto knife (or scalpel) on the first suture and gently work it down one side. Repeat for the other side. It may help to try and lever the partially freed vertebra away from the rest by twisting the blade slightly. Once you have separated the vertebra, repeat the process for the next one.

Notice how the neural canal rapidly expands in diameter in the sacral region. Indeed, it becomes so large that it encroaches upon the main body of each vertebra (called the **centrum**), which becomes reduced to a ring of bone. The reason for this expansion is explained in *The Sacral Swelling,* below.

The first few vertebrae have fairly prominent neural spines, but the next two or three have very short ones, and short transverse processes. These vertebrae will not be used, so go to the other end of the sacrum and start separating the ones with the prominent transverse processes.

Don't worry if some of the sacral vertebrae break during the process—you'll be very lucky if you can separate them all without some mishaps! Save all the vertebrae, including those that are not too badly broken—they can be repaired with glue when they are dry. You should finish up with half a dozen or more separate vertebrae on the wire, together with a few unseparated ones that will not be used. Label the string *sacral vertebrae,* noting which is the anterior end. Place it on the vertebrae plate.

## STEP 2: SEPARATING AND CLEANING THE BONES OF THE LEGS

Find the two legs—chances are the individual bones are still joined together by **ligaments** (tough sinews that connect bones to bones; **tendons** are similar, but they connect muscles to bones). Do the following for each leg:

# The Sacral Swelling

*Stegosaurus* (and several other dinosaurs) are often credited with having two brains: one in the usual place, and the other in the sacral region. Although untrue—these dinosaurs, like all other vertebrates, had only one brain—there was a considerable enlargement of the spinal cord in the sacral region. This is shown by the large size of the neural canals in the sacral region. In *Stegosaurus*, the partially fused sacral vertebrae form a bony cavity with a volume that is about twenty times larger than that of the braincase.

All tetrapods have a spinal enlargement in the sacral region, including humans, though these are nowhere near as prominent as in *Stegosaurus*. There is a second spinal swelling in the shoulder region.

The spinal column gives off paired spinal nerves, left and right, all the way down the vertebral column, and these exit between adjacent vertebrae. The spinal nerves are about the same thickness all the way down the backbone—almost as thick as a pencil in humans. However, they become enlarged and joined together in the shoulder and sacral regions, and the spinal cord is similarly enlarged. The reason for the increased complexity has to do with controlling the arms and the legs.

The usual explanation for the sacral swelling of the spinal cord in dinosaurs like *Stegosaurus* is that this area was associated with the nervous control of the massive back legs and spiked tail. However, this may be only part of the story. Birds, as you have seen for yourself, have an extensive sacral swelling, but this cannot be attributed solely to increased neurological function. In addition to housing the bird's spinal cord, the bony cavity accommodates a large structure called the **glycogen body,** of uncertain function. Perhaps the same was also true for some of its dinosaurian relatives.

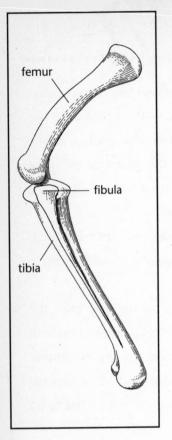

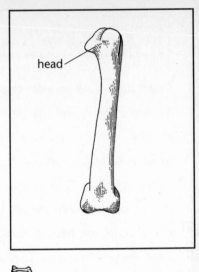

The bones of the left leg, in lateral view.

femur

fibula

tibia

head

The left femur, in anterior view.

1. Identify the femur (thighbone)—it is shorter than the tibia (shinbone). Keeping the two bones still attached at the knee joint, remove the meat from the femur. You'll notice a distinct knob at the upper end. This knob, called the **head of the femur**, fits into the hip socket.

   In adults, each end of the femur is formed of bone, but in young birds, it is made of cartilage. This cartilage forms a cap at each end of the bone, and provides for its growth. The extent of the cartilaginous cap therefore gives you an idea of the age of your particular chicken. For example, if the cartilage cap is large and easily comes away from the bone, you can be sure that you were eating a tender young chicken. You'll find similar caps at the ends of the tibia, too.

2. With the femur still attached, clear away the meat from the tibia, starting at the knee. Watch out for a slender bone, the fibula, which runs along the outside of the tibia. Once you've found the fibula, you'll be able to tell which leg you've got. This is because the fibula is always on the outside, and the head of the femur is always on the inside. Make a label to show which leg is which.

3. Remove the rest of the meat and other soft parts to separate the three bones (femur, tibia, fibula). Discard the tibia. Remove the cartilaginous caps from the ends of the femur. They may come off easily, but if not, remove them by scrubbing with the plastic scouring pad. If you've got an older bird, and the caps of cartilage do not come off easily with scrubbing, leave them attached. Clean and label the two femora and fibulae.

## STEP 3: SEPARATING AND CLEANING THE BONES OF THE WINGS

Find the remains of the two wings—chances are that the individual bones are still joined together by ligaments. Do the following for each wing:

Clearing away the meat as you go, identify the humerus (upper arm bone) and the two lower arm bones, the **radius** and the **ulna**. The radius is about half as thick as the ulna and is straight. At the far end of the lower arm you'll see a small projection—this is the bird's thumb, called the **alula**. The alula functions in flight as an antistalling device. You can often see the alula being deployed when watching pigeons coming in to

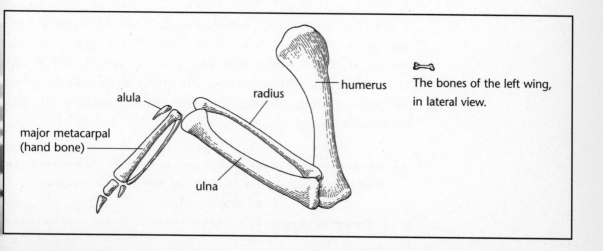

The bones of the left wing, in lateral view.

land. The alula, which looks like a small wing, pops out from the leading edge of the wing just before the pigeon lands.

Although you don't need to keep the chicken's thumb, you do need one of the two bones that lie next to the thumb. These bones, which are a little over an inch long (3 cm), are like the palm of our hand. These hand bones, called **metacarpals**, become fused together with maturity. One of the hand bones, the **major metacarpal**, is much thicker than the other, and is also straight. It is the only hand bone we need to keep. Discard the rest of the hand. Clean and label the bones that are needed, labeling them as *humerus, radius, ulna,* and *hand bone.* There is no need to distinguish left from right, except for the humeri.

## STEP 4: CHECKING THE SAUCEPAN FOR STRAY BONES

Unless you boiled a whole chicken, you'll find scraps of skin, meat, ligaments, and cartilage left behind on the bottom of the saucepan. But there may also be some bones that you've overlooked. Pour off most of the water, which will be cold, and feel through the scraps to find any stray bones. Check any bones that you find against the drawings to see whether they are needed.

### *Bone discoloration*

If any of your bones are discolored, they can be restored to a more natural bone white by using bleach. Make up an approximately 10 percent solution by adding half a cup of liquid bleach to one pint of cold water. Leave the bones to soak in the solution for about ten minutes. Rinse off under a running tap and leave them to dry.

**Warning:** Youngsters should not use bleach without an adult helper.

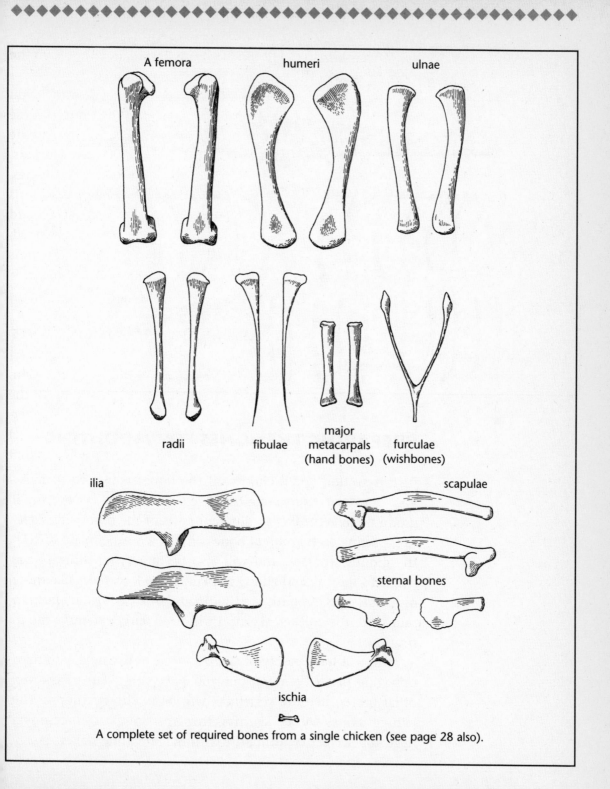

A femora   humeri   ulnae

radii   fibulae   major metacarpals (hand bones)   furculae (wishbones)

ilia   scapulae

sternal bones

ischia

A complete set of required bones from a single chicken (see page 28 also).

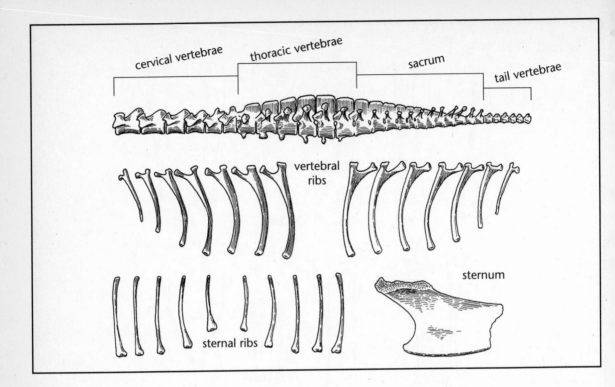

cervical vertebrae
thoracic vertebrae
sacrum
tail vertebrae
vertebral ribs
sternum
sternal ribs

## PREPARING THE BONES FOR MOUNTING

In this section you'll choose all the bones you need to make your dinosaur from your three sets of chicken bones. You'll group them according to different parts of the dinosaur's skeleton, placing each group of bones on its own paper plate to keep the groups separate. You will also be modifying some of the bones by cutting and gluing to make them look more like those of *Apatosaurus*. As birds are theropods, whereas *Apatosaurus* is a sauropod, the chicken skeleton will need fairly extensive modification.

You will have plenty of spare bones. For example, you need only one pair of femora, but you have three pairs. However, other bones, like the vertebrae, will be in shorter supply. The leftover bones will be kept together as spare parts, in case you have any accidents during the cutting and gluing stages.

# What Are Sauropods?

Sauropods, technically referred to as the Sauropodomorpha[1] (meaning lizard-foot form) or Sauropoda (the older term), are the giant **herbivorous** (plant-eating) dinosaurs. The group includes *Diplodocus*, *Brachiosaurus*, *Mamenchisaurus*, *Camarasaurus*, *Ultrasaurus*, and *Barosaurus*. Sauropods are characterized by their large bodies, solid, robust limb bones, relatively small skulls, long necks and tails, and dorsally placed **nares** (nostrils). The nares are sometimes positioned right on the top of the skull, as in whales. Other specialized characteristics include having 12–19 cervical vertebrae, each one about twice as long as it is high; 4–6 sacral vertebrae (the extra sacrals are to support the large body mass); a short, deep ilium; a reduced number of bones in the hand, with claws only on the thumb; and a femur that is longer than the tibia.

---

[1]Prosauropods are also included in the Sauropodomorpha.

## STEP 1: PUTTING THE BONES IN ORDER

1. Collect all the forked ribs together, left ones in one pile, right ones in another. There will be up to 18 for each side.

   If you are not sure which are left ones and which are right ones, check by picking up a rib and having a close look at it. Notice how curved it is. Also notice that the forked end has a long branch and a short branch. Lay the rib down on the table with the forked end farthest away from you and with the short branch touching the surface. The long branch will be pointing up toward you. Does the concave side of the rib face left or right? If it faces left, the rib is from the left side.

2. You need ten pairs of ribs for your dinosaur. Select them and arrange them according to size, as follows. The first ribs are small, increasing in size toward the middle of the rib cage,

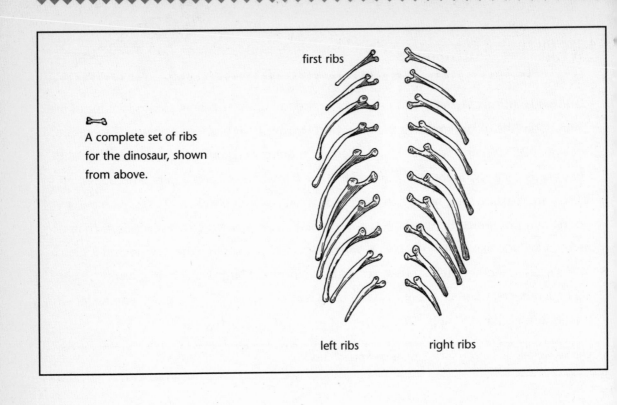

first ribs

A complete set of ribs
for the dinosaur, shown
from above.

left ribs                 right ribs

then getting smaller again. Using the illustration above as a
guide, choose your ten pairs of ribs and line them up on a
plate labeled *ribs*. Draw a line between the two sets, labeling
them *left ribs* and *right ribs*. Also label which is the first rib in
each set. Put any leftover ribs onto a paper plate labeled *spare
parts*.

3. Collect all the rest of the vertebrae together and put them
onto the vertebrae paper plate. There will be at least three
groups from each of the three chickens, labeled *neck and back
vertebrae, sacral vertebrae,* and *tail vertebrae*. Home-cooked
chickens will also probably have an additional string
labeled *anterior neck vertebrae* attached to the neck-and-back-
vertebrae string. Also add four of the six fibulae and the
three wishbones to the plate. These various bones will be cut
up and used as terminal tail vertebrae.

4. Put the three sterna onto a different paper plate and label it *skull*.

5. Put one pair of scapulae and one pair of sternal bones onto another plate and label it *shoulder*. Put the spare scapulae and sternal bones onto the spare parts plate.

6. Put one pair of ilia and two pairs of ischia onto a plate labeled *pelvis*. Add the leftovers to the spare parts plate.

7. Choose the thinnest pair of femora and put them onto a plate labeled *back legs and feet*. Put the shortest pair of hand bones and one pair of ulnae on the plate, too. Draw a circle about 2 inches (5 cm) in diameter and label it *back feet*. Find the sternal ribs, which are still on the ribs plate. Some of the sternal ribs are short—about ¾ inch or 20 mm long—and are straight. Choose twenty of these. Put ten inside the circle marked *back feet*; put the other ten to one side—they will be used for the front feet. Add one fibula to the back-legs-and-feet plate, too. Put the leftover bones onto the spare parts plate.

8. Choose one pair of humeri and place them on a plate labeled *front legs and feet*. Both humeri have to be shortened. Add one pair of hand bones (the shortest pair), and one pair of radii, placing the leftover hand bones and radii on the spare parts plate. Draw a circle about 2 inches (5 cm) in diameter, labeled *front feet*, adding the ten sternal ribs from the previous step. Add one fibula to the front-legs-and-feet plate, too. Put the remaining hand bones and radii onto the spare parts plate.

## STEP 2: MAKING THE DINOSAUR'S VERTEBRAL COLUMN

Before choosing the vertebrae for your dinosaur, you need to learn how they fit together.

# How the Vertebrae Fit Together

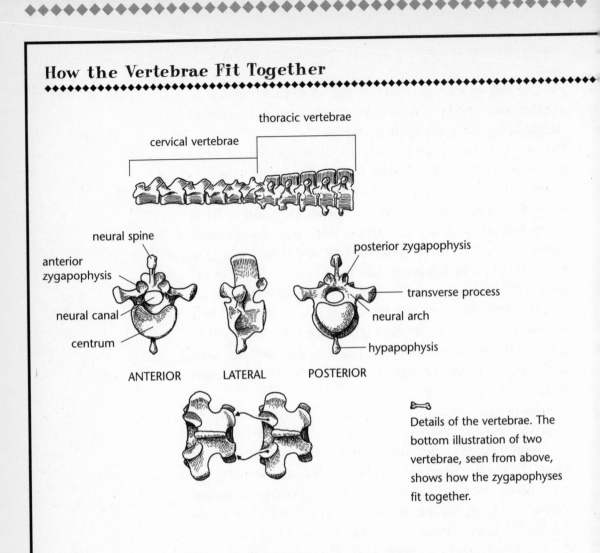

Details of the vertebrae. The bottom illustration of two vertebrae, seen from above, shows how the zygapophyses fit together.

Pick up one of the three strings of vertebrae from the vertebrae plate. Hold it with the neck end in your left hand and back end in your right hand. Look at the **thoracic** vertebrae, the ones to which the ribs were attached. These are easy to identify because each one has a large square bony plate, called the neural spine. There are only five thoracic vertebrae in birds, seven if you count the two vertebrae that were firmly attached to the anterior end of the sacrum. Humans, in contrast, have 12 thoracic vertebrae, while other mammals vary between 12 and 14. This gives birds a remarkably short back. Indeed, it is so short that their shoulders often touch their hips. As birds mature, their thoracic vertebrae fuse, and their backs become further stiffened by the development of long bony rods. This stiffening and shortening of the body all seems to do with their specialization for flight. Only the cervical vertebrae remain freely mobile, and birds are unusual in having 14 of these—we, like other mammals, have only half this number of neck vertebrae.

Notice how the plastic twist tie passes through the neural canal. The bone forming the canal is called the **neural arch**. Below the neural arch is the main body of the vertebra, the centrum. If you look at the centrum from the back (or from the front), you'll see that it has a double curvature, being curved from side to side as well as from top to bottom. This saddle-shaped surface (termed **heterocoelic**) is unique to birds.

Keeping the vertebrae still loosely strung on the plastic twist tie, try fitting two vertebrae together so that the saddle-shaped articular surfaces meet. Notice how snugly they fit. Pull the vertebrae apart again. Remember that the anterior (head end) of the vertebral column is toward the left, the posterior end to the right.

Look closely at the posterior end of the vertebra that is in your right hand. On either side of the neural arch, just above the neural canal, is a small round disc called a **zygapophysis.** Each disc faces down and out. Push the vertebrae together again. Notice how the posterior zygapophyses meet a similar pair on the anterior end of the other vertebra. Can you see which way the latter discs, the anterior zygapophyses, face? They face up and in. If you look down on the tops of the vertebrae as you articulate and separate them, you'll get a good view of the way the zygapophyses fit together. Their function is to help keep the vertebrae in line and to stabilize the vertebral column, while allowing movement. If you remember that the posterior zygapophyses, like bad gamblers, are always down and out (while the anterior ones face up and in), you'll always get the vertebra the right way round. While looking down on the thoracic vertebrae, notice the large processes that point laterally. These are the transverse processes, and they form part of the attachment for the ribs.

Try articulating a rib with one of the thoracic vertebrae, making sure you choose a rib from the appropriate side. The shortest branch of the fork (the tuberculum) articulates with the transverse process, while the long branch (the capitulum) fits into a round depression on the side of the centrum, close to the centrum's anterior edge.

Take a close look at the cervical (neck) vertebrae. They are characterized by their short, or nonexistent, neural spines. Their zygapophyses are also usually much larger than those of the other vertebrae. You should have between 4 and 6 cervical vertebrae. However, if you have a home-cooked chicken, you may have up to about 8 more cervicals on the string labeled *anterior neck vertebrae.* Try fitting two or three cervical vertebrae together. Are they all the right way round? If they are not, they'll never fit together properly. Just remember that the posterior zygapophyses always face down and out. Once you've got all the neck vertebrae lined up the right way, you are ready to choose the bones for your dinosaur's vertebral column.

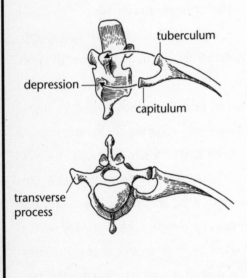

How the two branches of the rib articulate with the vertebra. Shown from the left side (top), and from the front.

◆◆◆◆◆◆◆◆◆◆◆◆◆◆◆◆◆◆◆◆◆◆◆◆◆◆◆◆◆◆◆◆◆◆◆◆◆◆◆◆◆◆◆◆◆◆◆◆

1. Cut a piece of plastic twist tie 20 inches long (50 cm) and make a small loop at the left end. This is for stringing your vertebrae as you choose them; the loop will hold them in place and mark the anterior end. Label this *backbone string*.

2. Find the three strings labeled *neck and back vertebrae*. Lay them on the table, one beneath the other, with their anterior (neck) ends facing left. Take a good look at them. Is each set about the same size as the others? If there are any obvious size differences, rearrange the three strings so that the top one has the smallest vertebrae and the bottom string the largest ones. Undo the twist ties at the anterior end. There should be about five neck vertebrae in each string, unless you have some additional cervicals on an anterior neck vertebrae string. There should also be five true thoracic vertebrae, plus the two vertebrae that were attached to the anterior end of the sacrum that are actually part of the sacrum.

   If you do have some of the anterior neck vertebrae, unfasten the twist tie and straighten it out, keeping the vertebrae still attached. Locate the anterior end of the sequence—this will be the end with the smallest neck vertebrae. Look carefully at the most anterior vertebra. Is it much shorter than the one behind it? Is its centrum pinched from side to side (that is, laterally compressed)? And does it have a pair of very prominent posterior zygapophyses (the anterior ones are minute in comparison)? If it matches up with all these features (check against the illustration), it must be the

ANTERIOR

posterior zygapophysis

LATERAL        POSTERIOR

The axis vertebra (the second cervical vertebra), seen from the left side and from the back.

**axis vertebra**, the second one in the entire neck series. When selecting the vertebrae for your dinosaur, choose only one axis vertebra, discarding any others. Arrange the string of anterior neck vertebrae so that the anterior end faces left. Attach the posterior end of that twist tie to the anterior end of the twist tie of the corresponding neck-and-back-vertebrae string. You will now have an essentially complete sequence of cervical vertebrae for this particular chicken. Remember that the cervical vertebrae are those that do not have square neural spines.

3. Starting with the top string, take the vertebra from the left and thread it onto the left end of the backbone string. Make sure that the anterior end of each vertebra faces left every time. Repeat for the next two strings. You now have three of your dinosaur's 15 cervical vertebrae on your backbone string.

4. Repeat step 3 until you have all 15 neck vertebrae (see illustration on page 35). Selecting vertebrae in sequence from these three strings is a good way of getting a gentle gradation in size. However, it may not work every time so you may need to change the order for some of the vertebrae. Just use your own judgment. If you have any leftovers, put them on the spare parts plate. If you have less than 15 vertebrae, you'll have to make up the number by including some thoracic vertebrae. To do this, go back to the three strings of vertebrae and take the first thoracic vertebra from the top string. Do the same for the other strings, until you have enough. Before adding these thoracic vertebrae to the cervical series, they have to be modified. Do this by following the instructions given in step 6 below.

When all 15 cervical vertebrae have been added to the backbone string, wrap a 4-inch (10 cm) length of plastic twist tie around the existing twist tie, to act as a marker. Make several turns with the marker, pulling tightly on the two ends to hold it in place. This shows where the cervical vertebrae end.

5. Count up the number of thoracic vertebrae that are still left on the three neck-and-back-vertebrae strings. You'll probably find that you've got 7 in each one. The first vertebra in each string will be the smallest one. You've got to choose 10 of these vertebrae for your dinosaur's back region and add them to the backbone string. These 10 back vertebrae should increase in size slightly, from first to last. If they are all about the same size, don't worry; that is all right, too. What you must avoid, though, is having the back vertebrae alternate in size between large and small.

6. Starting with the top neck-and-back-vertebrae string, take the first vertebra from the left. Before threading it onto the backbone string, you need to change its shape with a nail file. Notice that there is a small knob of bone at the base of most of the vertebrae (called the **hypapophysis**). File this off. Also, the neural spine is square and needs to be oblong, so file it down until it looks like the illustration. When you have finished filing down the vertebra, thread it onto the backbone string, making sure that the anterior end faces left. Repeat for the next two strings. You now have three of your dinosaur's back vertebrae. In reptiles, these are called **dorsal vertebrae** rather than thoracics and are the ones that lie between the pectoral and pelvic girdles.

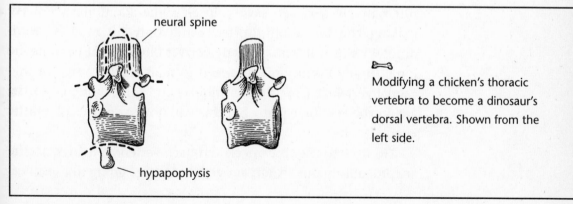

neural spine

hypapophysis

Modifying a chicken's thoracic vertebra to become a dinosaur's dorsal vertebra. Shown from the left side.

7. Repeat step 6 until you've got all 10 dorsal vertebrae. As before, you may need to use some judgment in the order in which you select the vertebrae, to be sure of getting a good gradation in size. Wrap a 2-inch (5 cm) length of twist tie around the backbone string to show where the dorsal vertebrae end. You'll have 3 or 4 vertebrae left over in each of the three strings.

8. Select five vertebrae from those remaining on the three neck-and-back-vertebrae strings. Choose the largest one first, based on the height of its neural spine, then the second largest, and so on. Before threading them onto the backbone string, change their shape by filing them down, as in step 6. Make sure that the anterior end of each vertebra faces left as you thread it onto the backbone string. You now have all five of your dinosaur's sacral vertebrae—the ones to which its pelvic girdle will be attached.

Wrap a 2-inch (5 cm) length of twist tie around the backbone string to show where the sacral vertebrae end and where the **caudal vertebrae** (tail vertebrae) will start.

At this stage you've got all of your dinosaur's vertebrae, except the ones for the tail. We now know that the tail of *Apatosaurus* ended in a long whiplash, with a total of about 80 caudal vertebrae. If you want, you can give your dinosaur a full-length tail. In this case you'll need 80 caudal vertebrae. Alternatively, you can save yourself some additional work by making the tail a bit shorter, using only 50 caudals. Your dinosaur will still look perfectly correct but will not be quite so long. In any event, you will need to manufacture some of the caudal vertebrae from the four fibulae and three wishbones that are on the vertebrae plate, but this will not be done until a little later.

Go back to the three neck-and-back-vertebrae strings. There are probably about six left altogether. You are going to use all of these vertebrae for the first part of your dinosaur's tail, but they first have to be arranged in order of decreasing size. Each vertebra also has to be filed down, too (see step 6). In addition to making the neural spines narrower, you should also file them so that they lean back slightly, as shown in the illustration on page 40. Thread the vertebra onto the backbone string, taking care that its anterior end faces left.

You've now got the first half dozen or so vertebrae of your dinosaur's tail. You've used up all those that were labeled *neck and back vertebrae* but still have all those on the vertebrae plate, namely three sets labeled *sacral vertebrae,* and three labeled *tail vertebrae.*

Take a good look at the sacral vertebrae. Notice that there are different kinds. The most anterior ones look like thoracic vertebrae, and have fairly prominent, rectangular neural spines and stout transverse processes. The next few vertebrae have progressively shorter neural spines and small transverse processes. These are not needed, and are probably still joined with their neighbors. After this, the transverse processes become progressively longer and stouter, and then become shorter again, but they remain stout. Notice that the transverse processes are initially single, but that they become double farther back. Untie the wires and do the following:

1. Put all the anterior sacral vertebrae with prominent neural spines together. You may have about 6 altogether. Arrange them in a row, in order of decreasing length of neural spine, with the largest ones at the left. Try to make sure that the anterior end of each vertebra faces left. To help with the orientation, you will probably be able to see a small notch on either side of the neural arch (for the exit of the spinal nerves; see the illustration on page 41). These are posterior in position.

2. Put all of the sacral vertebrae with single processes together—

you may have up to 9 of these. Arrange them in a row, in order of decreasing length of transverse processes, with the largest ones at the left. Make sure that the anterior end of each vertebra faces left. It's easy to see which way around the vertebrae go because the transverse processes slope toward the tail.

3. Repeat step 2 for the sacral vertebrae with the double transverse processes—you may have about 9 of these, too.

The sacral vertebrae now have to be modified. Proceed as follows:

1. Use the nail file to trim down the neural spine of the first group of sacral vertebrae. They should be given a slight backward slope, like the last vertebrae you added to the backbone string.
2. Using nail clippers, snip off one of the transverse processes from each of the sacral vertebrae—both the vertebrae with single and with double transverse processes. The remaining transverse process will become your dinosaur's neural spine.

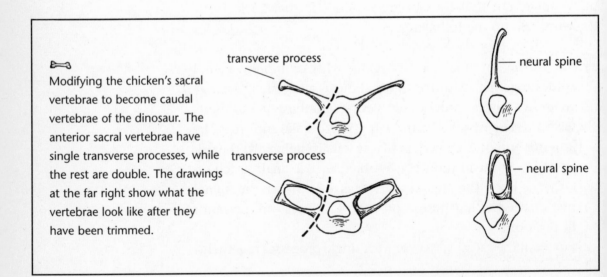

Modifying the chicken's sacral vertebrae to become caudal vertebrae of the dinosaur. The anterior sacral vertebrae have single transverse processes, while the rest are double. The drawings at the far right show what the vertebrae look like after they have been trimmed.

transverse process

neural spine

transverse process

neural spine

You are now ready to start threading the sacrals onto the backbone string.

1. Thread the sacral vertebrae with the prominent neural spines onto the backbone string, starting with the largest one.
2. Thread the sacral vertebrae with the single transverse processes onto the backbone string, starting with the vertebra with the longest process.
3. Thread the sacral vertebrae with the double transverse processes onto the backbone string, starting with the vertebra with the longest process.

Adjust the vertebrae so that their neural spines (the remaining transverse processes) line up with the neural spines of the other vertebrae. If some of the vertebrae are out of order in terms of the lengths of their neural spines, rearrange them. Tie a loop at the end of the twist tie to prevent the vertebrae's slipping off. This completes the backbone string. Count up how many caudal vertebrae you have so far (start counting from the last marker). You should have

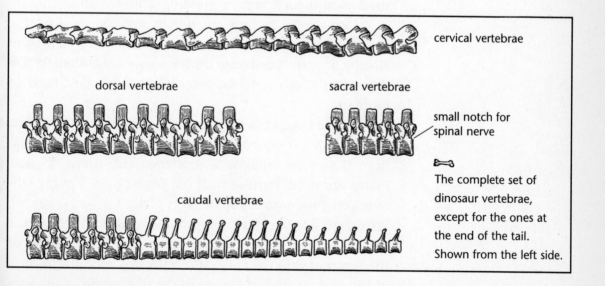

cervical vertebrae

dorsal vertebrae

sacral vertebrae

small notch for spinal nerve

caudal vertebrae

The complete set of dinosaur vertebrae, except for the ones at the end of the tail. Shown from the left side.

about 24. Now is the time to manufacture the terminal tail vertebrae from the bones remaining on the vertebrae plate.

Fill a saucepan with hot water, add the two pairs of fibulae and three wishbones from the vertebrae plate, bring them to a boil, and then let them simmer for about 20 minutes. Meanwhile, you can get on with the rest of the tail. (Don't worry if they simmer for a long time, they will not be damaged.)

Strip the plastic covering from a 16-inch (40 cm) length of twist tie (or a 10-inch length if you are opting for a shortened tail, i.e., a tail with 50 caudal vertebrae rather than 80). This will give you a length of wire for threading the last of your dinosaur's caudal vertebrae onto.

Twist one end into a small loop, to prevent the vertebrae's slipping off. You're now ready for the last part of the vertebral column.

1. Find the vertebrae labeled *tail vertebrae* on the vertebrae plate. There should be three groups of these (from the parson's nose of your three chickens), each containing at least six bones. Group them all together and arrange them in order of decreasing size—biggest one on the left. You will need all of them if you are building a full-length tail.

   Alternatively, to find out how many you need for the shortened tail, subtract the number of caudal vertebrae you already have threaded onto the backbone string from 35. (So if you had 22 tail vertebrae threaded already, you'd need 13 more.)

2. Discard the largest tail vertebrae, the ones that are very wide and flattened from front to back, as shown in the illustration. If you are building a shortened tail, count off how many you need, starting with the largest ones. Put the left-over vertebrae onto the spare parts plate.

3. Start threading the vertebrae onto the wire, starting with the largest one. Do this by piercing a small hole in the middle of the centrum with the end of the wire, just beneath the level of the neural canal, as shown in the illustration. If the wire

neural canal

DORSAL

LATERAL — neural spines

Selecting vertebrae from the chicken's tail for use in the dinosaur's tail. Discard wide vertebrae *(top left)*, pierce the remaining vertebrae *(top right)*, and thread them onto a wire, in order of decreasing size *(middle and bottom)*. *Note:* Not all of the caudal vertebrae that are needed for the full-length tail are shown.

does not puncture the bone easily, pop it into boiling water for a few minutes and try again. Make sure that the vertebrae always face toward the loop at the end of the wire. You can tell which way they face, because their (stubby) neural spines are inclined toward the back.

You now need to do something with the bones that have been simmering. There are more than you need for the job, but this will give you a lot to choose from, and it won't matter if you make some mistakes when cutting them.

If you are building a full-length tail, proceed as follows:

1. Remove one wishbone from the water. Using the nail clippers, cut off a 20 mm length from one of the free ends and discard it. Cut off four 5 mm lengths from the wishbone. If possible, cut one more 5 mm long piece. (If you have problems with pieces of bone flying everywhere, try cutting them inside a plastic bag.)
2. Repeat step 1 for the other side of the wishbone, discarding the part in the middle where the two halves join.
3. Repeat steps 1 and 2 for the other two wishbones.

Terminal vertebrae, made from wishbones and fibulae. *Note:* Not all of
the caudal vertebrae that are needed
for the full-length tail are shown.

ANTERIOR

4. Remove two of the fibulae from the water and cut each of them into 6 or more rods, each 5 mm long, discarding 15 mm or so from each end.

5. Repeat step 4 for the other two fibulae, but cut them into 4 mm long segments.

6. Arrange your cut pieces of bone in order of decreasing length and thickness, as illustrated. You should have more than 40 of them. Determine how many you need to complete your dinosaur's tail—remember there are 80 caudal vertebrae.

If you are building a shortened tail, proceed as follows:

1. Remove one wishbone from the water. Using the nail clip-pers, cut off a 20 mm length from one of the free ends and discard it. Cut off three 6 mm lengths from the remaining wishbone. If possible, cut one more piece, 5 mm long. (If you have problems with pieces of bone flying everywhere, try cutting them inside a plastic bag.)

2. Repeat step 1 for the other side of the wishbone.

3. Repeat steps 1 and 2 for a second wishbone.

4. Remove one fibula from the water and cut it into a series of rods, each 5 mm long, discarding 15 mm or so from each end.

5. Repeat step 4 for a second fibula, but cut it into a series of rods each 4 mm long.

6. Arrange your cut pieces of bone in order of decreasing length and thickness, as seen in the illustration on page 43. You should have more than 20 pieces. Determine how many you need to complete your dinosaur's tail—remember that you are using only 50 caudal vertebrae.

When you've got a nice string of "vertebrae" that decrease in size evenly, thread them onto the wire with the rest of the tail vertebrae, starting with the largest one. Try to get a gentle transition between the tail vertebrae already on the wire and the new ones. This can be achieved by carefully selecting the vertebrae. It may be necessary to change the order of one or two of the tail vertebrae that are already in place. The rods of bone should thread onto the wire without difficulty, but if you have problems, try soaking them in hot water for a few minutes, then try again. The bones should fit loosely on the wire. If they are too tight, enlarge the hole in the middle of the bone by slipping it up and down on the wire. Return any excess soaked bones to the spare parts plate.

Bend the end of the wire into a loop to prevent the vertebrae's slipping off. Label this string of vertebrae *tail string* and place it on a plate with the backbone string.

You've now got all your dinosaur's vertebrae. Take courage—this was the largest job of the whole project and the rest will go much faster.

## STEP 3: PREPARING THE FRONT LEGS, BACK LEGS, AND FEET FOR CUTTING

In this section you will be marking all the bones that have to be cut with penciled cut marks. As each set of bones is marked up, you'll put them into their own plastic sandwich bag, to prevent confusion. You'll also add a label to each bag, identifying which dinosaur bones it contains.

The chicken's humerus and femur have to be reduced in length, because both bones are relatively shorter and broader in sauropods. Their stockier proportions are largely due to the enormous weight a sauropod's limbs had to carry, and also because they had a more lumbering gait.

Find the paper plate labeled *front legs and feet*. The first bone to be marked up is the humerus.

## Hollow Bones

Most of the bones you cut up are hollow, and you'll see that many of them are filled with marrow. This red bone marrow, as it is called, is where the red blood cells (and certain others) are manufactured. Red bone marrow is especially extensive in young animals and occurs in most bones. However, with maturity, the number of manufacturing sites decreases, and the red bone marrow becomes converted into a yellow fatty material. In times past we used to crack open the limb bones of the animals we hunted to extract the yellow fatty material, called tallow, for making candles.

Although most tetrapods have some hollow bones, the skeletons of birds are characterized by their extreme hollowness. Some of the spaces, as we have seen, are occupied by red bone marrow, but others are air-filled. Some of the bones, notably the humerus and many of the vertebrae, have openings that lead into the hollow spaces within. Birds' skeletons are said to be **pneumatic**, a feature they share with other theropods and with sauropods.

In addition to having air-filled bones, birds have a complex system of air sacs and ducts that communicate with the lungs. The birds' air-sac system is part of their **respiratory** (breathing) system and functions to maintain a one-way flow of air through the lungs. This type of airflow is unique to birds. Other animals, ourselves included, have a two-way airflow through the lungs—the air flows in and then out again.

### The Humerus

Find the pair of humeri. Each humerus has to be shortened by removing a segment of the midshaft. Do the following:

1. Look at the bones. You'll see that one end of the humerus is wider than the other. The wide end is the upper end. Pencil

an arrow on the wide upper end, pointing toward that end of the bone.

2. Hold the humerus vertically, with the narrow end against the table and the wide end pointing up toward you. Notice that one surface is convex (curved outward, like a ball) while the other is concave (curved inward, like a bowl). The concave surface faced forward during the chicken's life.

3. Place each humerus flat on the table, concave surface down. You'll find that the bones lie flat on the table (if you flipped each over so that its convex surface was against the table, it would rock). Lay them side by side with their wide ends at the top. Notice the large opening, called a **pneumatic foramen**. This opening faced inward during the chicken's life. Therefore, if you lost the labels telling you which was left and right, you could work it out for yourself. Notice the prominent crest on the opposite edge to the pneumatic foramen. This process is called the **deltopectoral crest**.

4. Turn over the humeri so that the concave side of the upper ends face you. The bones will not lie flat. Write *anterior* across the wide upper end of each bone to remind you which side will face forward in your dinosaur skeleton.

5. Turn over the humeri again so that the convex surface is toward you. Your dinosaur's humeri need to be 36 mm long. Measure the length of one of the chicken's humeri and subtract 36, which leaves the amount to be removed. Cut a strip of paper to this length (or use the dividers), and lay this along the shaft of the humerus, moving it up and down until the widths of the shaft are about the same at either end. This will ensure that the two cut ends match up afterward. When satisfied with the position, pencil two horizontal marks across the shaft. Also draw a vertical line down the length of the bone, marking the posterior surface. Repeat for the other humerus.

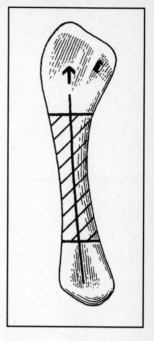

Marking up a chicken's humerus to become a dinosaur's humerus. This is a left humerus in posterior view.

## Flying Muscles

The deltopectoral crest of the bird's humerus provides an extensive attachment area for the pectoral muscles. These are usually the largest muscles in a flying bird's body and function to drive the wings downward during flight. Most of the white meat we carve from the breast of chickens and turkeys is the pectoral muscle.

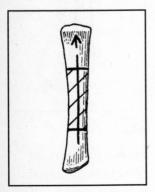

Marking up a chicken's hand bone (major metacarpal) to become a dinosaur's radius.

### The Radius

Find a pair of hand bones. Each one will become a dinosaur's radius (one of the lower bones of the front leg). Do the following for each one:

1. Look at each end of the bone. Notice that one end is thicker and looks more square than the other. This chunkier end will be the upper end of the dinosaur's radius. Lay the bone on the table, with the upper end pointing away from you. (It doesn't matter which surface lies on the table, but you'll probably find that the bone lies more steady one way than the other.) Mark the upper end of the bone with a heavy penciled arrow, pointing away from you.
2. Draw a heavy pencil line down the middle of the bone. Measure 12 mm from each end and draw a heavy pencil line across the bone. These are cut marks.

   Put the two bones into a plastic sandwich bag. Label the bag *radius*. Set the bag aside for later.

### The Ulna

Find a pair of radii. Each radius will become a dinosaur's ulna (one of the lower bones of the front leg). Do the following for each bone: Look at each end of the chicken's radius. Notice that one end is rounded while the other end is flat. The rounded end will be the upper end of the dinosaur's ulna. Mark this direction with a penciled arrow. Measure 24 mm from this rounded end and draw a heavy pencil line across the bone. This is a cut mark.

Put both bones into a plastic sandwich bag and add a label, *ulna*.

## Feet

As the feet are small, the individual bones that make them up are readily lost. Consequently, the entire assembly of each foot will be completed in this section. You have a choice of making simple feet or realistic-looking ones. Whichever ones you choose will require softening the bones in boiling water and cutting them. To avoid small pieces of bone flying everywhere, do the cutting inside a plastic sandwich bag. The front and hind feet are treated in exactly the same way for the simple feet, and there are only minor differences for the detailed feet. Work on one pair of feet at a time, starting with the back feet.

### Simple Feet

Find the ten sternal ribs and one fibula in the circle labeled *back feet* on the back-legs-and-feet plate. Boil the bones in water for about five minutes, allow them to cool, and then proceed as follows.

Select the five longest sternal ribs and cut each one in half. This will give you two sets of bones, one for each foot. Dry the bones. This can be done within minutes if you warm them using a 60-watt table lamp (see page 50). Otherwise, leave them to air-dry for about an hour. Do the following for each set of five foot bones.

1. Make a plasticine ball ⅝ inch (15 mm) in diameter. Flatten the ball onto a paper plate to make a disc that is about ¾ inch (20 mm) in diameter and ¼ inch (5 mm) thick.

Marking up a chicken's radius to become a dinosaur's ulna.

Making simple feet from sternal ribs. The back feet are the same as the front ones, and there is no distinction between left and right.

2. Press the cut ends of the foot bones into the plasticine in a semicircular pattern. They must be firmly embedded. Slope the bones inward, toward the center of the disc, with their top ends in contact with one another.

3. Using a toothpick, run a thin thread of glue across the tops of the bones. Run a second and thicker thread lower down, running across the anterior surfaces of the upper ends of the bones.

    Allow the glue to set for several hours before removing the feet from the plasticine.

Repeat the whole sequence for the bones labeled *front feet,* on the front-legs-and-feet plate. Put one pair of feet onto the plate labeled *back legs,* the other onto the plate labeled *front legs.*

## Realistic Feet

With minor differences (noted below), the front feet are constructed the same way as the back ones. As in the case of the simple feet, begin by finding the ten sternal ribs and one fibula in the circle labeled *back feet* on the back-legs-and-feet plate. Boil the bones in water for about five minutes and allow them to cool. Divide the ten sternal ribs into two sets that are evenly matched in terms of size. This is done by putting the largest element into the first set, a similarly sized one into the second set, the next smallest one into the first set, and so on. You will fin-ish up with two sets of five sternal bones. Take one set of sternal bones and proceed as follows:

1. Make a ball of white plasticine, about 1½ inches (40 mm) in diameter. Shape the ball into a flat-topped cone, with sides sloping at an angle of about 45°.
2. Select the three largest bones, measure 10 mm from the rounded ends, and cut, using the nail clippers. Be sure to make all cuts square, otherwise the individual toe segments will not fit together properly. The other two sternal ribs should be cut to a length of 7 mm. Do not exceed these lengths, otherwise the feet will be too large. Save all the left-over pieces. Dry the bones, either using a lamp or in the air. Lamp drying only takes ten or fifteen minutes, but you should air-dry for about an hour.
3. Arrange the five bones, cut ends uppermost and touching, around the top of the plasticine cone, as shown in the illus-

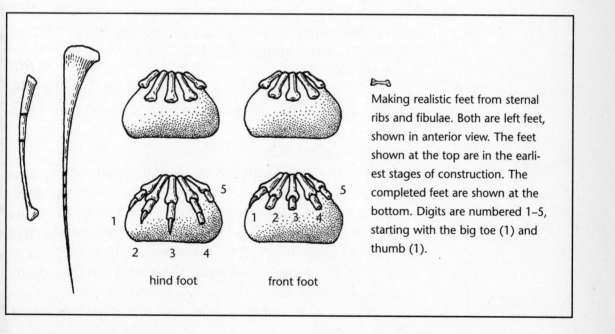

hind foot        front foot

Making realistic feet from sternal ribs and fibulae. Both are left feet, shown in anterior view. The feet shown at the top are in the earli-est stages of construction. The completed feet are shown at the bottom. Digits are numbered 1–5, starting with the big toe (1) and thumb (1).

tration. Splay them out in a semicircle, with the shortest bones at the two ends. Stick them to the surface of the plasticine using minimum pressure (to make them easier to remove). They should be inclined at about 45° to the vertical.

4. Using the remaining pieces of the sternal ribs, cut two sections, each about 3 mm long, and three sections that are 5 mm long. Place these in contact with the ends of the bones that are already set in plasticine, the two short sections being aligned with the toes at the two extreme ends. Make sure the bones are in contact and that there are no gaps.

5. By cutting some of the bone scraps at an acute angle, make three pointed triangles of bone that are about 5 mm long. You may want to use the fibula for this. These pointed bones will be the claw of the big toe (designated digit 1), and the next two adjacent toes (designated digits 2 and 3).

6. With the partially constructed foot facing you, designate the toe at the extreme left as digit 1. Mark this in plasticine below the toe. Write in the numbers of the remaining toes (digits 2 through 5), digit 5 being at the extreme right. Place the claws on the ends of digits 1–3, the three toes on the left. This makes it a left hind foot, because the clawed toes are on the inside.

   Cut a section of bone from a sternal rib, about 3 mm long. Position this at the end of digit 4 (next to the third clawed toe).

   Write *left hind* on the plasticine.

7. Repeat steps 1–5 for the second set of five sternal ribs.

8. With the partially constructed foot facing toward you, designate the toe at the extreme right as digit 1. Mark the numbers of the five toes in the plasticine, as before, ending with digit 5 at the far left. Place the claws on the ends of digits 1–3, the three toes on the right. This makes this foot a right hind one, because the clawed toes are on the inside.

   Cut a section of bone from a sternal rib, about 3 mm

long. Position this at the end of digit 4 (next to the third clawed toe).

Write *right hind* on the plasticine.

9. Make sure the two hind feet are the same size and shape. It might be necessary to do some trimming of some of the bones if some digits are too long.

The front feet are made the same way as the back feet, the only difference being that there are fewer bones, with only one claw. Begin by finding the ten sternal ribs and one fibula in the circle labeled *front feet* on the front-legs-and-feet plate. Repeat all of the steps in construction of the back feet, with the following changes.

Once the ring of five cut-down sternal bones have been attached to the plasticine cone (end of step 3), cut five 3 mm long sections of bone. Place these at the ends of the five bones. Each finger is comprised, therefore, of only two bones. Cut a narrow triangle of bone about 5 mm long. With the hand facing toward you, place this claw, which belongs to the thumb, at the end of the finger at the far left. This is now a left hand. Write *left fore* on the plasticine.

The right hand is made in the same way, but with the claw placed at the end of the finger at the far right. Write *right fore* on the plasticine. Make sure that the two forefeet are the same size and shape, making any adjustment.

## Gluing the Feet

Glue each of the four feet in the following way, using Krazy Glue and clear glue.

◆◆◆◆◆◆◆◆◆◆◆◆◆◆◆◆◆◆◆◆◆◆◆◆◆◆◆◆◆◆◆◆◆◆◆◆◆◆◆◆◆◆◆◆◆◆◆◆◆

**Caution:** Krazy Glue is toxic. It can cause serious damage if it comes into contact with your eyes, so safety glasses should be worn. Krazy Glue readily bonds with skin. It should not be used by youngsters.

◆◆◆◆◆◆◆◆◆◆◆◆◆◆◆◆◆◆◆◆◆◆◆◆◆◆◆◆◆◆◆◆◆◆◆◆◆◆◆◆◆◆◆◆◆◆◆◆◆

1. Taking great care not to get glue on your person, gently squeeze a partial droplet of the liquid from the end of its nozzle and touch it against each bone joint. The idea is to get the liquid to run into the crack between the two contact edges of the bones (by capillary action). Krazy Glue will not bridge a gap, but it will join two bones together if they are in contact. Do not worry if the Krazy Glue leaks over the surface of the two bones being joined. However, you do not want it running onto the plasticine where it will solidify as an extension of the toes, so go sparingly. When satisfied that all the joints have been glued, proceed to the next step.

2. Using a toothpick, apply a thread of clear glue across the fronts of the top ends of the upper foot bones to consolidate the Krazy Glue joints. You can also use some clear cement to consolidate any of the other foot joints that may look in need of attention. However, go very sparingly with the cement and only apply it to the joint surfaces.

   Leave the feet for several hours for the cement to set.

3. After the glue has set, carefully remove each foot from the plasticine. This is best done by undercutting each toe with an Exacto knife and gently prodding and coaxing it free. Be patient, and the foot will eventually come free. If any of the bones come loose, they can be reglued by placing them into contact with one another and touching them with a small droplet of Krazy Glue.

You now have to remove the excess plasticine and do some additional gluing. Do the following for each foot.

1. Lay the foot on a flat surface with the underside facing you. Taking each toe in turn, hold the upper bone firmly with forceps. This will steady the entire toe, allowing you to pare away at the plasticine with an X-Acto knife. If there are any solid webs of Krazy Glue attached to the bones, they can be snipped off with nail clippers. I had some extensive webs of

rock-hard glue on some of the toes of my dinosaur and despaired of ever removing it. However, I was pleasantly surprised at how easily it snipped off, without any damage to the tiny bones.

As the plasticine is white, and since it is on the underside of the foot, it will not show. Therefore, you don't have to remove every last trace. However, the more you can clean off, the more effectively you will be able to consolidate the joints.

2. Using a toothpick, and with the underside toward you, apply small beads of clear cement to any of the joints that are not already well glued. Even if none of the joints need attention, run a thread of glue between the ends of the upper bones, as you did on the top of the foot.

At present your dinosaur appears to have very flat feet. However, this will be put right when they are mounted on the skeleton.

You can now continue preparing the leg bones for cutting, finding what you need on the plate labeled *back legs and feet*.

## *The Femur*

Find a pair of femora. Each femur has to be shortened by removing a section from the middle of the shaft. Shortening, as noted earlier, makes the proportions of the femur more like those of a sauropod. It also straightens out the femur, removing the curvature of the shaft that is characteristic of theropods. The chicken, remember, is a theropod, whereas *Apatosaurus* is a sauropod, and that group does not have a bowed femur.

Do the following for each femur.

1. Look at the two ends of the bone. Notice how porous they are. This is because the bone is immature and shows that there was a cartilaginous cap. The bones of some hatchling

## Heavy-Duty Feet

Elephants weigh several tons, all of which has to be borne by their feet, which are adapted to deal with the heavy load. If you looked at the skeleton of an elephant, you would see that they appear to walk on their toes. However, in life, there is an extensive rubbery pad supporting the toes. This pad, which is remarkably resilient, absorbs much of the impact of their footfalls, just like a well-cushioned running shoe. The bottom of an elephant's foot is therefore round, without separate toes, and makes a rounded footprint.

Sauropod dinosaurs similarly left rounded footprints in the ground, some of which hardened into fossil trackways. Their foot skeleton was also like that of the elephant, the toes being short and widely splayed. We can therefore be quite confident that they too walked on their toes, with an extensive pad of soft material to cushion the load. In some sauropods, including *Brachiosaurus* and *Camarasaurus*, the metacarpals (palm of hand) and metatarsals (sole of foot) were positioned almost vertically. In *Apatosaurus* the metacarpals were nearly vertical, but the metatarsals were inclined at an angle.

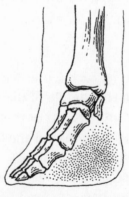

The foot of an elephant, shown from the side. Notice that they appear to be walking on tiptoe, but their toes are supported by a spongy pad, shown by the dotted area.

dinosaurs have a similar appearance, for similar reasons. One end of the femur has a pair of condyles (a double knob). This is the lower, or knee, end of the bone. If you look carefully, you'll see that one of these condyles is slightly shorter and

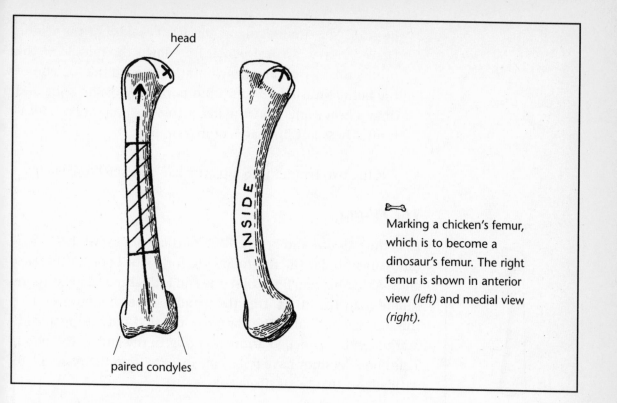

head

INSIDE

paired condyles

🦴

Marking a chicken's femur, which is to become a dinosaur's femur. The right femur is shown in anterior view *(left)* and medial view *(right).*

thicker than the other. This shorter condyle is on the inside of the femur. Look at the other end of the femur. When viewed end-on, this end appears to be triangular, with a condyle, the head of the femur, on the inner side. Mark the head of the femur with an *X*. Mark the femur with a letter *R* for right or *L* for left. (Even if you'd lost the labels saying which side they were, you could easily work it out for yourself. You know that the head of the femur, which you've marked with an *X*, is at the top of the bone, and is on the inside—that is, it faces toward the hip.) Write *inside* on the inside edge of the femur.

2. Lay the femur down, with the upper end pointing away from you, so that the two condyles rest on the table. The shaft of the bone will curve toward you, away from the table (you'll find this is the only position in which the femur will

lie still). You are looking at the front surface of the femur. Draw a heavy, vertical pencil line down the middle of the front surface, with an arrow pointing toward the top end of the bone. Measure 23 mm from both ends of the bone and draw a heavy line, horizontally, across the bone at both locations. These last lines are cut marks.

Put the two femora into a plastic bag and label it *femur*.

### The Fibula

Find the pair of hand bones. Each of these bones will become a dinosaur's fibula. Do the following for each: Look at the two ends. As before, you'll see that one end is thicker and looks more square than the other. This thick end will be the lower end of the dinosaur's fibula. The flatter, wider end is the upper end. Mark it with a penciled arrow pointing to the end of the bone. This bone does not have to be cut, so leave it on the paper plate with a label that reads *fibula*.

### The Tibia

Find a pair of ulnae. Each one will be cut and modified into a single tibia. Do the following for each bone.

1. Look at the two ends. One is wider and thicker than the other. This wide end will become the upper end of the dinosaur's tibia. Lay the ulna flat on the table with the thick upper end pointing away from you. Run your finger along the upper half of the shaft of the bone, all the way to the top. Can you feel a small depression that starts about ½ inch (1 cm) from the thick end? If necessary, turn the bone over so that this depression faces you. Draw a heavy pencil line down the middle of the bone, marking the top end with an arrow pointing to the thick upper end, as shown in the illustration.
2. Notice that the shaft is curved. Does the convex side point

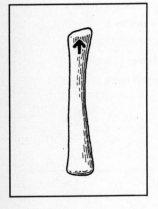

Marking a chicken's hand bone, which is to become a dinosaur's fibula.

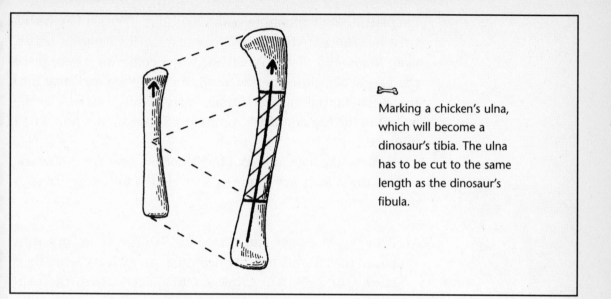

Marking a chicken's ulna, which will become a dinosaur's tibia. The ulna has to be cut to the same length as the dinosaur's fibula.

toward the left or the right? If it points toward the right this bone will become the dinosaur's right tibia.

Find the dinosaur's fibula (an unmodified chicken hand bone). Measure its length. This will also be the length of the dinosaur's tibia. Divide this length in half and measure this distance from both ends of the ulna. Draw a thick, horizontal line across the shaft at these points. They are cut marks. Therefore, if the length of the dinosaur's fibula were 34 mm, you would measure 17 mm from each end of the ulna.

Put the marked-up bone into a plastic bag with a label that reads *tibia,* noting whether it is left or right.

Repeat steps 1 and 2 for the other ulna.

## STEP 4: PREPARING THE FRONT AND BACK LEGS FOR GLUING

Boil some water in a saucepan. While you are waiting for the water to boil, add about half a cup of hot tap water to each of

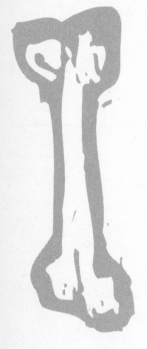

the plastic bags containing bones to be cut. Tie each bag with a twist tie. There are five bags altogether, labeled *humerus, radius, ulna, femur,* and *fibula.* When the water comes to a boil, place the plastic bags into the saucepan. As you place each bag into the saucepan, stab it several times with a knife. This will let the air out of the bag and the hot water in. Let the bones boil for 15 minutes.

Remove the bags and cool them under a cold tap. Allow the bags to drain for a few minutes, then do the following for each one:

1. Remove the bones and the label. Dab the bones dry with paper towels and put them onto a paper plate with their label. Using the nail clippers, cut squarely across the penciled cut marks. Take care not to cut at an angle, as this will make it difficult to join the cut ends together afterward.

   For four of the dinosaur's bones—the femur, humerus, radius, and tibia—you'll be cutting out the center piece. Discard these. For the other bone, the ulna, you'll be cutting off and discarding the longest end; the piece you keep is marked with an arrow.

   Don't worry if the bones do not cut cleanly because they can be filed down later. Save any broken pieces—you may be able to put them back in place right away, while the bone is still soft and damp.

2. Leave the bones to dry thoroughly before gluing. There are two ways of doing this. You can either do this within about half an hour, by using a table lamp, or you can leave them overnight to air-dry. To use the fast method, simply adjust the lamp so that it shines horizontally, then place the bones on the inside of the shade. Alternatively, you can put the bones directly onto the bulb. Provided it is no brighter than 60 watts, it will not scorch the bones until several minutes have passed, but keep an eye on them.

   You'll probably find that boiling the bones has made the

pencil marks much fainter. If this is the case, pencil over the marks again when the bones have dried.

## STEP 5: GLUING THE BONES OF THE FRONT AND BACK LEGS

Paleontologists use large boxes filled with sand to hold bones in a vertical position while glue is setting. You can do the same by filling some empty cans with sand. This is the best method, but as an alternative, you can use a strip of plasticine instead. Stick a strip of plasticine, about 4 inches (10 cm) long, 1½ inches (4 cm) wide and ½-inch (1 cm) thick, onto the tabletop. After you have glued bones together, press them, vertically, into the plasticine and leave them to set. If you decide to use the plasticine method, read "plasticine strip" for "sandbox" in the sections that follow.

The methods for gluing the leg bones of your dinosaur are similar to those used for mending full-size dinosaur bones. Follow these instructions for each of the leg bones to be glued— these are the humerus, radius, femur, and tibia.

1. Test-fit the two halves by bringing their cut ends together. Make sure that the pencil line is on the same side for each half. File off any jagged edges with the nail file.

   **Note:** When gluing the femur, you'll probably find that the cut ends fit together best when one half of the shaft is rotated relative to the other. The two halves of the pencil line will therefore no longer be in line.
2. The largest bones, the humerus, femur, and tibia, need some internal supports, namely, a small piece of toothpick. Break off a piece of toothpick, about three-quarters the length of the bone to be joined. Sharpen both ends with the Exacto knife. Push one end of the toothpick halfway into one of the cut ends, making sure it goes in straight. Hold the other half

of the bone in line with the first half, so that its cut end is about 1 mm from the free end of the toothpick. Now push the two ends of bone together, so that the toothpick penetrates the other half of the bone.

The two halves of the bone should fit together properly and be in line. If they are not in line, pull them apart and try pushing them together again. If they are still not lined up properly, you can try removing the toothpick and start over again. If you still don't have any luck, you can try enlarging the hole for the toothpick, using an intact toothpick.

Pull the two halves of the bone slightly apart—just enough to squeeze in some clear glue. Apply the glue to both ends of the bone and allow it to dry for a few moments. Then push the pieces of bone firmly together.

3. Stick one end of the glued bone into the sandbox so that it stands up. Make sure that the bone has a label beside it. Let the glue dry for about an hour. The radius doesn't need the toothpick treatment. Simply add a drop of glue to each cut end, let it dry for about a minute, then push the two ends together.

4. Draw a line down the middle of a paper plate. Put the left femur on one side of the line, together with the left tibia and a fibula. Repeat on the other side of the line for the right femur, right tibia, and a fibula. Label the plate *back legs,* noting which is left and right.

5. Take a second plate and draw a line down the center. On one side place a humerus, a radius, and an ulna. Do the same on the other side. Label the plate *front legs,* noting which is left and right.

## STEP 6: FILLING IN THE CRACKS IN THE GLUED LEG BONES

Because the fit between the ends of the bones that you glued will not be perfect, there will be some gaps across the joins.

# Repairing and Conserving Fossil Dinosaur Bones

Fossil dinosaur bones are glued in a way similar to the method used here, though we never grind away bone to make a better fit. Instead, we look for contact surfaces between the broken ends of bones and glue these together. The same clear cement used here is used for the smaller bones, but large bones are usually repaired with epoxy cement. Sometimes bones have to be reinforced with steel rods, especially the larger ones, and this involves drilling them out first. Any gaps are usually filled in with plaster, which is often painted afterward, sometimes color-matched to the bone. Although color-matching is more aesthetically pleasing, it is far better to paint the plaster a slightly different shade or even to leave it unpainted. This allows researchers to distinguish between real and restored bone when they are taking measurements.

Fossil bone is often described as being petrified (turned into stone), but this is a misunderstanding caused by its appearance. Bone is naturally porous, and the small spaces often become filled in with minerals during preservation, causing the fossil bone to look like stone. However, much of the original bone material usually remains, including its microscopic structure. Some of the original organic compounds may also be preserved, including some of the amino acids that were part of its protein molecules.

Fossil bone is often treated with various preservatives. If the bone is porous—as, for example, in all of the Canadian dinosaurs in my museum—it is impregnated with certain clear varnishes, such as Vinac and Gelvar. This not only strengthens the bone, but also protects the surface from flaking and cracking. These plastic solutions can be applied with a paintbrush. Alternately, the bone can be vacuum-impregnated by immersing it in the solution inside a pressure chamber, which is then evacuated. As the air is pumped out of the chamber, it bubbles out of all the small spaces within the bone. When the pressure is restored, the varnish replaces the displaced air. The bone is left to dry for a day or more, during which time the solvent evaporates, leaving a thin film of the plastic on the surfaces of all the pores that were penetrated.

There may also be some broken edges that will need filling. These repairs are made in the following way.

1. Mix up one level teaspoon of Spackle, or plaster of paris, with a few drops of cold water in a paper cup to make a thick paste.
2. Using the wide end of a toothpick, apply some of the plaster to the gaps in each of the leg bones. Push the plaster deep into the cracks. It doesn't matter if there is a ridge of extra plaster around the crack because this will be removed later—but try not to smother the bone in plaster! Take particular care not to cover any of the penciled labels on any of the bones. Wait for ten minutes, then wipe off the excess plaster with a tissue.
3. Put a small dab of plaster on the cut end of each ulna, just to finish it off.
4. Leave the plaster to dry for about 15 minutes. If it doesn't feel dry at the end of this time, leave it until it does.

Add a few drops of water to one end of a Q-Tip and squeeze it dry. Using the damp tip, wipe off the dried plaster from the surface of the bones—but avoid wiping the actual cracks.

## STEP 7: PREPARING THE PELVIS FOR CUTTING

Find the paper plate labeled *pelvis*. *Apatosaurus*, as mentioned earlier, is a sauropod or "lizard-hipped" dinosaur, and has a three-pronged pelvis. The upper prong is the ilium and below it is the pubis (in front) and the ischium (behind). You'll build the dinosaur's pelvis in two halves, starting with the left half.

Find the ilium—there is a left one and a right one. Also find the ischium—there are two pairs. You'll use the chicken's ilium for the dinosaur's ilium, but it will have to be trimmed down in length. This is because sauropods have a short, deep ilium, whereas birds, being theropods, have a relatively long one. The chicken's ischium has to be shortened, too.

You'll use a chicken's ischium for the dinosaur's pubis. This is because a bird's pubis is slender (in adults it is fused with the ischium), whereas sauropods have a short, stout pubis. As a chicken's ischium is different from a sauropod's pubis, it will have to be trimmed to the right size and shape.

All of the bones have to be marked up and boiled prior to cutting, so make sure the cut marks are thickly penciled.

Start with the left side of the pelvis.

1. Find the left ilium. Lay it down flat on the table (if you try and lay it down on its other side it will not be stable). When the ilium is lying flat, you are looking at it from the outside. The front of the ilium faces toward the left. Run a finger along the lateral (outside) surface. Notice that the anterior part of the ilium is hollow, while the posterior portion bulges out toward you. (If it's the other way around, you've got the ilium from the right side—swap it with the other ilium and start again.)

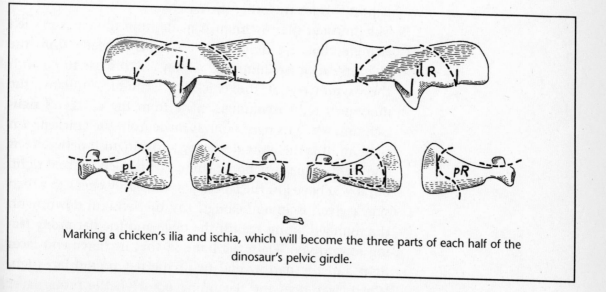

Marking a chicken's ilia and ischia, which will become the three parts of each half of the dinosaur's pelvic girdle.

2. Find the short prong that points downward and draw a vertical pencil line on it. Measure 17 mm from this pencil line toward the front of the ilium and make a pencil mark. Draw a curved line from this mark to the top of the ilium, as shown in the illustration. Measure 21 mm from the vertical pencil line toward the posterior end of the ilium and make a pencil mark. Draw a curved line from this mark to the top of the ilium (as shown in the illustration). This last curved line will follow the curve of the bulge of the back part of the ilium. Mark the ilium with the letters *il* for ilium and *L* for left.

3. Repeat steps 1 and 2 for the other (right) ilium. Mark it with the letters *il* for ilium and *R* for right. Put the two ilia into a plastic bag with a label marked *pelvis*.

4. Find the four ischia. Look at one. Notice that there is a flat, triangular blade and a narrow part that branches into two short prongs. One of the prongs is round, and the other is flat. The flat prong is easy to hold between your finger and thumb and is a convenient way of holding the bone while you are marking it with the pencil for subsequent cutting. This flat prong will eventually be cut off. Draw a bold pencil line all around the base of the flat prong (as a cut mark). Repeat this for the other three ischia.

5. The dinosaur's left ischium is made from the chicken's left ischium, but the dinosaur's left pubis is made from the chicken's *right* ischium. The reason for this has to do with the asymmetry of the chicken's ischium. Similarly, the dinosaur's right ischium is made from the chicken's right ischium, while its right pubis is made from the chicken's *left* ischium. It is therefore necessary to distinguish between left and right ischia. The bones should be labeled left and right, but if you have lost the labels, you can easily check to which side a given ischium belongs. Lay the ischium down, with the rounded prong against the table and the flat prong facing toward you. Place the bone so that its flared end faces right and the narrow end (with the flat prong) faces left. Which way does the flat prong point? If the prong faces

downward, the ischium is from the right side. If the prong faces upward, the ischium is from the left side. Label each ischium accordingly.

6. Hold a right ischium by the flat prong so that the flat prong is farthest away from you. Measure 27 mm from the round prong toward the widest end. Make a pencil mark on the bone, and draw a curved line across the blade, passing through this mark, as shown. Mark the bone with a letter *p* for pubis and *L* for left.

7. Hold a left ischium by the flat prong and measure 26 mm from the round prong toward the widest end. Make a pencil mark on the bone and draw a curved line through it, as shown in the illustration. Mark the bone with a letter *i* for ischium and *L* for left.

8. Hold a right ischium by the flat prong and measure 26 mm from the round prong toward the widest end. Make a pencil mark on the bone and draw a curved line across the blade passing through this mark, as shown in the illustration. Mark the bone with a letter *i* for ischium and *R* for right.

9. Hold a left ischium by the flat prong and measure 27 mm from the round prong toward the widest end. Make a pencil mark on the bone and draw a curved line through it, as shown in the illustration. Mark the bone with a letter *p* for pubis and *R* for right.

10. Put the dinosaur's left ilium, left ischium, and left pubis into a plastic bag labeled *pelvis, left side*. Do the same for the right side.

## STEP 8: PREPARING THE SHOULDERS FOR CUTTING

Locate the paper plate labeled *shoulder*. Find a pair of scapulae (shoulder blades), the longest bones, and a pair of sternal bones. The latter will be made into your dinosaur's coracoid bones. The chicken's scapula has to be shortened because this bone is somewhat more robust in sauropods than in theropods. The chicken's coracoid cannot be modified into your dinosaur's coracoid because birds have specialized coracoids, which has to do with flying. The chicken bone that is closest in shape to a sauropod's coracoid is the sternal bone.

Both the scapulae and the sternal bones have to be cut down in length. Start with the scapulae.

1. Take a look at the left scapula. You'll see that one end, the posterior end, is flat, while the anterior end is thick. Lay the bone down so that the thick anterior end faces left. Notice that the thick end has a knob that faces toward you (if it faces away from you, then you've got the two scapulae reversed. Swap for the other scapula and start again).

   Measure 45 mm from the tip of the anterior end toward the posterior end and make a pencil mark. Draw a heavy, curved line across the blade of the scapula, as shown in the illustration. Mark the bone with the letters *s* for scapula and *L* for left. These pencil marks are on the outside of the scapula.

2. Repeat step 1 for the right scapula, but lay it down so that its anterior end faces right. Mark the bone with the letters *s* for scapula and *R* for right. Place both scapulae in a plastic bag labeled *shoulder*.

3. Examine one of the sternal bones. Notice that there is a thick half-rounded part and a narrow prong. Draw a thick line

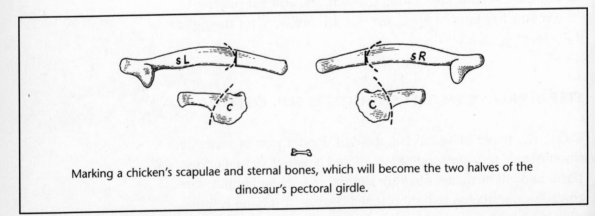

Marking a chicken's scapulae and sternal bones, which will become the two halves of the dinosaur's pectoral girdle.

across the base of the prong, so as to continue the shape of the half-round part, marking a semicircle. Mark with the letter *c* for coracoid.

4. Repeat step 3 for the other sternal bone and put both of them into the plastic bag with the other shoulder bones. (No distinction is made between left and right coracoids.)

◆◆◆◆◆◆◆◆◆◆◆◆◆◆◆◆◆◆◆◆◆◆◆◆◆◆◆◆◆◆◆◆◆◆◆◆◆◆◆◆◆◆

**Warning:** Youngsters should be supervised when boiling water.

◆◆◆◆◆◆◆◆◆◆◆◆◆◆◆◆◆◆◆◆◆◆◆◆◆◆◆◆◆◆◆◆◆◆◆◆◆◆◆◆◆◆

5. Bring some water to a boil in a saucepan. While you wait for the water to boil, add about half a cup of hot tap water to each of the plastic bags, closing them with a twist tie. When the water in the saucepan is boiling, add the plastic bags, stabbing each one with a knife, as before. There are three bags, labeled *pelvis, left side*; *pelvis, right side*; and *shoulder*. Let the bones boil for 15 minutes.

6. Remove the bags and cool them under a cold tap. Drain off the water. Taking care not to lose the labels, open the bags and take out the bones. Dab the bones dry with tissue and put them on a paper plate with their labels.

7. Using the nail clippers, cut along the pencil lines. Don't forget to cut the flat prongs from the ischia. Allow the bones to dry thoroughly, either by using a lamp or by leaving them to air-dry for a couple of hours.

8. When the bones are dry, smooth off all sharp corners and edges with the nail file. Check each of the bones against the illustrations, doing any final shaping with the file.

## STEP 9: GLUING THE PELVIS

Each half of the pelvis is made up of three bones: the ilium, the pubis, and the ischium. You're going to glue one side of the pelvis at a time, starting with the left side, so collect together the three bones that are marked *L* for left.

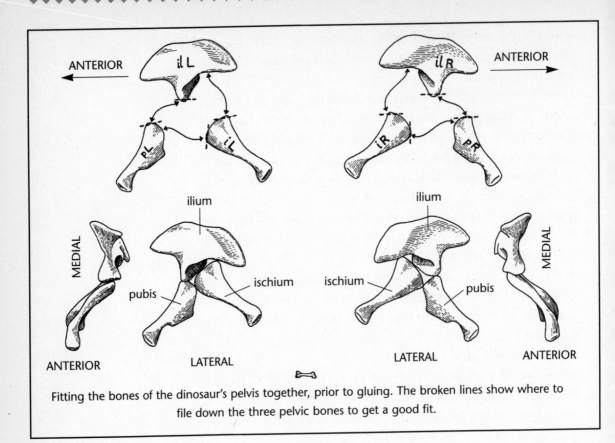

ANTERIOR ←

il L

il R

ANTERIOR →

PL

i L

i R

PR

ilium

ilium

MEDIAL

pubis

ischium

ischium

pubis

MEDIAL

ANTERIOR

LATERAL

LATERAL

ANTERIOR

Fitting the bones of the dinosaur's pelvis together, prior to gluing. The broken lines show where to file down the three pelvic bones to get a good fit.

1. Look at the illustration, which shows how the three bones of each side of the pelvis fit together. Notice that you'll have to file some small flat areas on the pubis and ischium so that the three bones fit together properly. Have your sandboxes handy for assembling each half of the pelvis. If you are using plasticine instead of a sandbox, you need to make it into a flat-topped cone like the one used for making realistic feet (see page 51). This will allow you to tilt the pubis and ischium downward relative to the ilium (step 8 below) without burying them in plasticine.

2. Line up the three bones of the left side, as shown in the illustration. You'll find that they don't fit together very well. Carefully file away a small, flat area from the top front corner

of the pubis, as shown in the illustration. Be *gentle* with the bone, because it is brittle and easily broken. Don't file very much off; try fitting the pubis so that the flat area you've just filed fits up against the prong of the ilium. It may be necessary to file a little more off the pubis to get a good fit.

3. Carefully file a small, flat area off the top front corner of the ischium, as shown in the illustration. Try fitting the ischium so that the flat area you've just filed fits up against the pubis. You may have to file a bit more off the ischium to get a good fit.

4. Carefully file a small, flat area off the top of the back corner of the ischium, as shown in the illustration. Try fitting the ischium again, to check how well the flat area you've just filed fits up against the ilium. You may need to file a little more off to get a better fit. The ischium should now fit in the gap between the pubis and ilium, but if the gap is too large, file some bone off the end of the ilium's prong. This will narrow the gap.

5. Once all three bones fit together properly, they're almost ready for gluing. But before doing this, you need to fit together the bones of the right side.

6. Look at the illustration and repeat steps 2–5 for the right side of the pelvis.

7. Check the distance between the tips of the pubis and ischium for each side. Adjust the bones until the distances are the same for both sides.

8. The three bones of each half of the pelvis are lying flat in a sandbox, and while this is all right for the ilium, the other two bones need to slope downward. Do this by gently pushing the ends of the pubis and ischium 5 mm down into the sand.

9. Use a toothpick to apply a bead of clear glue to each of the places where the individual bones of the pelvis meet. Use enough glue to run down between the cracks. Leave the two halves of the pelvis to set for an hour.

10. When dry, apply more glue to the other side, to consolidate the joints. Leave the bones to set for at least an hour.
11. Remove any remaining pencil marks, using the nail file or the X-Acto knife.

## STEP 10: GLUING THE SHOULDER

1. Find the left scapula (labeled with the letters *s* and *L*) and one of the coracoids (labeled with the letter *c*).
2. Hold the scapula in your right hand so that the pencil marks face you, with the thick anterior end pointing to the left. Put a finger of your left hand on the tip of the thick end of the scapula. This will be the part that is glued to the coracoid.
3. Examine the coracoid. Notice that there are essentially three edges, a thick edge, an intermediate edge, and a thin edge

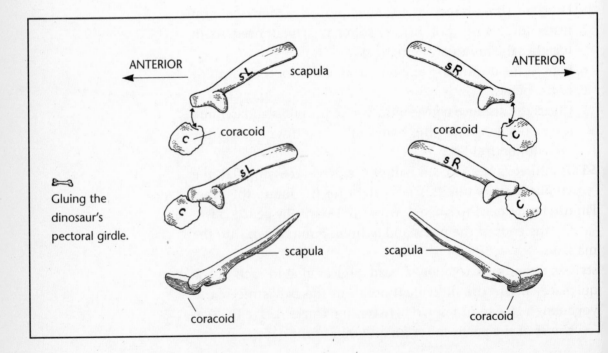

Gluing the dinosaur's pectoral girdle.

(which has to be cut across). Notice also that there is a small concave depression, about 4 mm long, in the middle of the intermediate edge. Hold the thin part of the coracoid between the finger and thumb of your left hand, so that the thickest part points away from you and to the right. Add a droplet of Krazy Glue to the concave depression in the intermediate edge. If you prefer, you can use clear cement instead of Krazy Glue.

4. Still holding the coracoid in your left hand, pick up the scapula in your right hand so that the pencil marks face you, with the thick part of the bone pointing to the left. Press the tip of the scapula into the droplet of glue, angling the coracoid so that its inside surface faces obliquely upward— viewed from the front, they make an obtuse angle (greater than 90°) to one another, as shown in the illustration. Press the two bones firmly together. When they are firmly joined (which should take less than a minute), add a droplet of clear cement to the joint from the other side, and leave the bones to set for an hour.

5. Repeat steps 1–4 for the right scapula and the remaining coracoid, making sure that you substitute *right* for *left* (and vice versa) in the instructions.

6. Clean off any remaining pencil marks and put the two sides of the pectoral girdle on a plate marked *shoulders*.

## STEP 11: PREPARING THE SKULL FOR GLUING

Find the paper plate labeled *skull*.

Given its small size and the limitations imposed by the materials and equipment available, it is only possible to build a stylized model of a sauropod skull. However, it will still look quite realistic by the time you are done, and it will finish off your skeleton very nicely.

You only need two sterna for making the skull; the third one

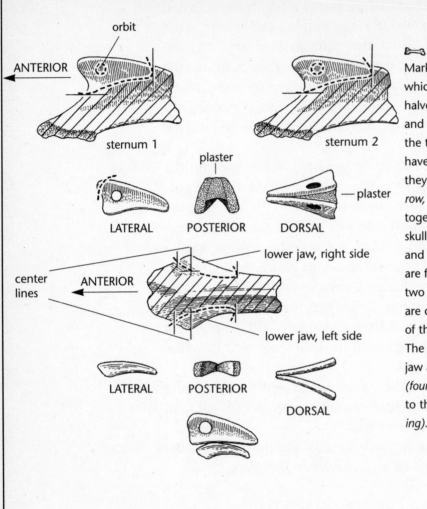

orbit

ANTERIOR

sternum 1

sternum 2

LATERAL  POSTERIOR  DORSAL

plaster

plaster

center lines

ANTERIOR

lower jaw, right side

lower jaw, left side

LATERAL  POSTERIOR

DORSAL

Marking the two sterna, which will become the two halves of the dinosaur's skull and lower jaws *(top)*. Once the two sides of the skull have been cut and dried, they are filed down *(second row, left)*. Once glued together, the back of the skull *(second row, middle)* and top *(second row, right)* are filled with plaster. The two halves of the lower jaw are cut from the two edges of the sternum *(third row)*. The two halves of the lower jaw are glued at their tips *(fourth row)* and then glued to the skull *(bottom drawing)*.

is there to give some choice. Each sternum will be used for making one side of the skull. Lay each sternum down on its right side so that the anterior end of each one faces left, as shown in the illustration. Look carefully at the shape of the anterior end of the keel. This will become the back of your dinosaur's skull. Choose a pair of sterna that look most similar in shape. Proceed as follows:

1. Hold one of the sterna with the anterior end facing left. Measure 25 mm from the anteriormost tip of the keel, toward the posterior end, and draw a vertical pencil line. This marks the length of the skull. Also measure down 10 mm from the top edge of the anteriormost tip of the keel, and draw a horizontal line. This marks the depth of the skull. Draw in the outline of the skull, as shown in the illustration. Use heavy pencil lines, otherwise they may wash off in step 6 below.

2. Draw in the outline of the **orbit** (eye socket), as shown in the illustration. Its center should be 10 mm from the anteriormost tip of the keel, and its diameter should be 5 mm.

3. Repeat steps 1 and 2 for the second sternum, making sure that the two halves look the same.

4. Using the points of the nail scissors, bore a hole through the center of each orbit. **Important**: Make sure you place the point of the scissors exactly at the center of the orbit. Bore right through the bone. Keep on making the hole bigger, until it is the same size as the penciled outline of the orbit. Do the same on the other side of the bone so that the diameter is the same on both sides.

5. Lay one of the sterna on the table with the anterior end facing left, in preparation for drawing in the two halves of the lower jaw. Draw two vertical lines, as shown in the illustration, that pass through the widest point of the sternum. These lines are called center lines. Draw two more vertical lines, 5 mm anterior of the center lines. Measure 5 mm from the edge of the sternum along each center line and make a small mark to show the depth of the lower jaw. Measure 20 mm from the two anteriormost vertical lines and draw two more vertical lines. These show the length of each half of the lower jaw. Draw in each jaw. If you like, you can draw in a second set of jaws on the other sternum to have in reserve.

6. Boil the two bones in a saucepan for ten minutes, then run them under a cold tap to cool them off. Shake off the excess

water. Cut around the outline of the skull. It is probably easiest to do this roughly, with scissors, than to follow the outline more accurately with the nail clippers. Don't worry if you can't cut right to the line—this can be fixed later with the nail file.

Also, don't worry if your cutouts break—they can be repaired later, too. Do the same for the lower jaws.

7. Leave the two sides of the skull and lower jaws to dry thoroughly, either using a lamp or leaving them to air-dry for several hours.

8. Using the nail file, trim the bone to the pencil line and smooth off any rough edges. Also smooth out the curvature of the back of the head at about the level of the orbit. The bones are fragile *so be gentle*. Glue any broken pieces together.

9. Prop the two halves of the skull up in a sandbox. The tips of the two halves should be just touching, but the back ends should be about 12 mm apart (from outside to outside). Slope the top edges of the two halves together, so that they touch, from about the level of the orbits to the tip of the snout. Some careful filing along the contact edges of the dorsal region of the snout will help achieve this end.

10. Using a toothpick, run a thread of clear cement along the contact edges of the two halves of the skull and leave to dry for an hour. Alternately, touch a droplet of Krazy Glue to the contact edges between the two halves of the skull. Check to see that the two sides are firmly glued together. Then turn the skull over and run a thread of clear cement to the inside seam, to consolidate the union. Leave to dry for an hour in an inverted position.

11. When the skull has thoroughly dried, mix up a half-teaspoon of Spackle, Polyfilla, or plaster of paris—it should be as thick as toothpaste. Using the flat end of a toothpick, apply the plaster to the seam between the two halves of the skull. Continue the in-filling around the back of the skull, but only

go down about halfway, otherwise you will not be able to attach the skull to the wire support during the final assembly.

12. Examine each half of the lower jaw. The narrowest end is anterior, the dorsal surface is convex, and the ventral surface is concave. Notice that the thickest part of the jaw is ventral and posterior in position. Try fitting each half of the jaw to the skull. File a small flat area at the point where it contacts the skull.

13. Place the two halves of the lower jaw upside down in a sand-box, with their tips touching but their posterior ends splayed apart. The space between their posterior ends should correspond to that between the posterior ends of the skull. When satisfied that the jaws are properly aligned, add a droplet of Krazy Glue to the tip. Wait one minute and check to see that the two halves are joined together. Gently lift up the glued jaws and hold them against the skull to check that the two line up correctly. Also check that the two halves of the jaw are properly aligned with each other. If you're dissatisfied, gently separate the pieces and repeat the procedure. If you prefer, you can use clear cement instead of Krazy Glue.

14. Once the two halves of the lower jaw have been glued satisfactorily, place them in position upon the inverted skull. Use a small piece of plasticine at the tip of the snout to obtain a satisfactory gap between the upper and lower jaws. Adjust until the skull looks realistic, then apply small droplets of Krazy Glue to the contact surfaces, using a toothpick. This is just to tack the lower jaw in position, so be very sparing with the glue. (Again, you can use clear cement instead of Krazy Glue.)

15. Check to make sure the jaw is securely attached, then examine the skull right side up. Once satisfied with its appearance, use a toothpick to add small droplets of clear cement to the inside surfaces of the contact edges, thereby consolidating the union.

## MAKING THE WOODEN BASE AND METAL SUPPORTS

### STEP 1: MAKING THE METAL SUPPORTS

1. Cut three pieces of wire from a metal coat hanger, as shown in the illustration, using the pliers. Try not to bend the wires as they are cut. Two of the pieces are each 4½ inches long (11 cm), the third is 14 inches (36 cm) long. The two short

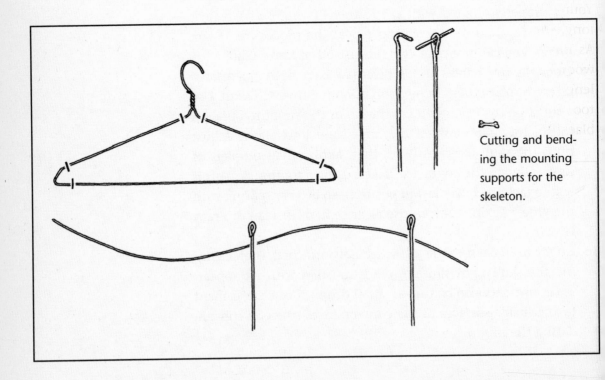

Cutting and bending the mounting supports for the skeleton.

pieces are for the vertical supports; the long one is for the backbone support.

2. Take one of the short pieces and choose the end that is the least straight (if there is one). Using the pliers, bend the last ⅜ inch (1 cm) over at a right angle. Now bend this right angle over a piece of leftover coat hanger to form a loop. Remove the leftover piece of coat hanger.

3. If necessary, straighten up the vertical part of the wire.

4. Repeat steps 2–3 for the second short piece of coat hanger.

5. Bend the long piece of coat hanger into the curve shown in the drawing. This is the backbone support. Wrap a piece of floral tape around the tail end, as shown in the illustration, to remind you that this is the back end.

## STEP 2: MAKING THE WOODEN BASE

Your piece of wood for the base should be about 2 feet (60 cm) long, 5 inches (13 cm) wide, and preferably ¾ inch (2 cm) thick. As noted earlier, some hardware stores sell finished pieces of wood of the appropriate size, described as "craft board." A length of wooden molding of the appropriate width works well, too. For an added touch, you can varnish the base or paint it black.

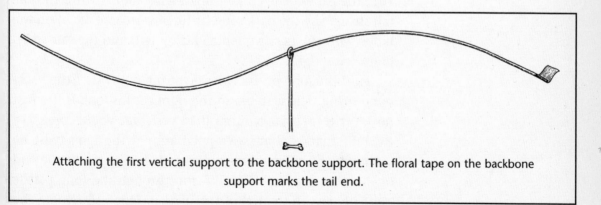

Attaching the first vertical support to the backbone support. The floral tape on the backbone support marks the tail end.

## ASSEMBLING THE SKELETON

### STEP 1: MOUNTING THE VERTEBRAE

In this section you'll be threading the individual vertebrae onto the horizontal backbone support, and attaching this to the two vertical supports. From the illustration on page 81, you can see which is the top of the backbone support, so you can thread the vertebrae the right way up. Make sure you keep the vertebrae in line with one another.

1. Thread the front end of the backbone support (the end farthest from the floral tape) through the loop of one of the vertical supports. Push it through the support until it extends 7 inches (18 cm) beyond the loop, temporarily holding it in place with a small length of floral tape. This front part of the backbone support is for the dinosaur's neck. Check to make sure that this will be long enough by holding the neck section of your backbone string (the first 15 vertebrae, up to the first twist tie marker) against the backbone support. Add on an extra 15 mm for the attachment of the skull. Adjust the position of the vertical marker accordingly. Make sure you've got the backbone support lined up properly—remember that the concave part of the neck curve faces upward.

2. Find the paper plate containing the backbone string and the tail string. Lay the backbone string of vertebrae down on the table, with the neck vertebrae facing left, and the tail vertebrae facing right.

   Find the loop of the twist tie at the left end of the backbone string. The vertebra to the right of this loop is the first neck vertebra. If you count off 15 vertebrae you'll come to a twist tie marker that is wrapped around the long twist tie upon which the vertebrae are threaded. This marks the end of the neck region. Carefully snip through the long plastic twist tie, just to the left of the marker. This will free up the last neck vertebra.

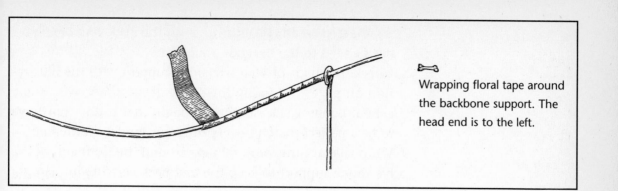

Wrapping floral tape around the backbone support. The head end is to the left.

3. Cut off a 3-inch (8 cm) length of floral tape. Wrap this tightly around the wire backbone support at the base of the neck, working your way toward the head end. Aim to cover about 2 inches (5 cm) of the wire. This will give the vertebrae something to grip and stop them from jiggling.

4. Remove the last (fifteenth) neck vertebra from the backbone string. Making sure not to change the direction in which it is facing, thread it onto the backbone support and push it all the way up to the vertical support. The vertebra may feel tight when you are slipping it onto the backbone support because of the thickness of the floral tape—but it needs to be a snug fit. Rock it from side to side as you push it along the backbone support. If it really is too tight, unwrap the floral tape and rewrap it more tightly. If this still doesn't work, just use less floral tape. If the vertebra is too loose, use more floral tape.

5. Repeat step 4 for the fourteenth, thirteenth, and twelfth neck vertebrae, in their turn. When adding the vertebrae, make sure that they interlock properly. That is, make sure that the zygapophyses at the front of a vertebra articulate with the corresponding zygapophyses at the back of the next vertebra.

6. Wrap another 3-inch (8 cm) length of floral tape around the wire, starting where you added the last tape. Add the next four neck vertebrae.

7. Repeat step 6 and continue until all the neck vertebrae have been added to the backbone support.

8. Check the shape of your backbone support with the illustration on page 81. Modify the shape, if necessary, with some careful bending. Please note, though, that it does not have to be a perfect match—every dinosaur model is different.

9. Wrap several turns of floral tape around the front end of the backbone support to keep the first neck vertebra in place.

At this point you've threaded all of the cervical vertebrae onto the backbone support. You've now got to repeat the process for the next 15 vertebrae on the backbone string. The first 10 of these are the dorsal vertebrae (called thoracic vertebrae in birds and mammals); the next five are sacral vertebrae.

1. Wrap a 3-inch (8 cm) length of floral tape around the backbone support, immediately behind the vertical support.

2. Remove the marker twist tie from the backbone string to free the first dorsal vertebra. Also, remove the floral tape from the tail end of the backbone support, as well as the tape that was temporarily holding the vertical support in place.

3. Thread the first dorsal vertebra onto the backbone support, making sure not to change the direction in which it is facing. Push this vertebra as close as possible to the vertical support in front. It is important that the dorsal vertebrae be firmly attached and do not rock from side to side. If the attachment is not firm enough, use more floral tape. Add the second, third, and fourth dorsal vertebrae, making sure they interlock—as you did for the neck vertebrae. The first vertical support should now be firmly held in place—by the neck vertebrae in front and the dorsal vertebrae behind.

4. Wrap another 3-inch (8 cm) length of floral tape around the wire, starting from the last piece of tape, and add the next four vertebrae.

5. Add four more vertebrae (the last two dorsal vertebrae and

the first two sacral vertebrae). Remember that all the vertebrae have to be firm. If they are not, add more floral tape.

6. Repeat step 4 and add the last three sacral vertebrae.
7. Remove any excess floral tape from the backbone support and add the second vertical support. Wrap some floral tape around the loop of the vertical support and the backbone support, tying them firmly together. There will be about 1½ to 2½ inches (4–6 cm) of backbone support left projecting beyond the loop of the vertical support.

The five sacral vertebrae will be used for the attachment of the pelvis, just as they were in the real dinosaur. And, like those real-life bones, the sacral vertebrae need to be firmly joined together. In the real dinosaur, the bones were fused together, just as they were in the chickens you dissected, but here we're going to use glue. Lay the vertebral column on its side and add droplets of clear cement to the joins between adjacent centrums. Use sufficient glue to firmly unite the sacral vertebrae, but don't smother them! Allow the glue to set for a half hour, then turn the column over and repeat the gluing process on the other side.

At this stage you've got all the vertebrae mounted except for those of the tail. There are two sets of tail vertebrae. The first ones—those closest to the pelvis—are still on the backbone string. The last tail vertebrae, which includes the small ones right at the tip of the tail, are on the tail string. You've now got to start mounting the tail vertebrae.

1. Wrap a 3-inch (8 cm) length of floral tape around the backbone support, immediately behind the second vertical support.
2. Making sure not to change the direction in which it is facing, thread the first tail vertebra onto the backbone support. Push this vertebra as close as possible to the vertical support. Add the next two or three tail vertebrae, leaving about 6 or 7 mm of the backbone support projecting beyond the last one.

3. You now need to attach the pipe cleaner to the backbone support. Do this by pushing one end of the pipe cleaner through the gap between the last vertebra and the backbone support upon which it is threaded. It might be a bit of a tight squeeze, but you should be able to push the end of the pipe cleaner at least ½ inch (1 cm) along the backbone support. If you have difficulty, you can take off the last vertebra, pass the end of the pipe cleaner through its neural canal, and then rethread it onto the backbone support. Tightly bind the end of the pipe cleaner to the end of the backbone support with a length of floral tape. (If you like, you can cement the pipe cleaner to the backbone support with Krazy Glue, but still wrap the joint with floral tape because this makes it much easier to thread on the next few tail vertebrae.) The floral tape also stops the vertebrae from slipping.

4. Add more tail vertebrae, one at a time as before. Use more floral tape to keep them tight, but you will soon get to the point where you no longer need it. If the vertebrae become difficult to thread onto the pipe cleaner, try rocking them from side to side as you push them on. You'll use up all the tail vertebrae on the backbone string, and will need to start using those on the tail string.

   You'll find that the vertebrae get harder to push on as you get toward the end of the pipe cleaner, because they're getting smaller. But don't push them too hard, otherwise they will break. When you're at the point where you can't add another vertebra, cut the pipe cleaner flush with the end of the last one you added, and go on to the next step. At this point you will probably have mounted about 20 tail vertebrae.

5. Measure a 14-inch (35 cm) length of twist tie (7½-inch [20 cm] length if you are building a shortened tail) and strip off the plastic covering. Bend the last 10 inches (25 cm; 5½ inches for the shortened tail) of the wire into a curve, which will become the end part of the tail. Leaving the first 5 mm bare, tightly wrap about one inch (2.5 cm) of floral wrap around the

next inch (2.5 cm) of the straight part of the wire.

6. Start threading the remainder of the tail vertebrae onto the curved end of the wire. Start with the largest vertebra, moving it all the way along the covered wire until it just reaches the bare wire. Make sure that the anterior end of this first vertebra faces toward the bare end of the wire.

   Continue until you have added all the vertebrae you need, adding or removing floral tape as necessary, ending with the thinnest one. The floral tape should stop them from rocking from side to side. Add a dab of glue to the wire just before adding the last tail vertebra. When the glue has set and the last vertebra has stuck, snip off the end piece of the wire.

7. Attach this last tail section to the rest of the tail by pushing the bare piece of wire into the gap between the last tail vertebra and the pipe cleaner. The final adjustment to the curvature of this last tail section can be made later, when the backbone has been attached to the wooden base.

## STEP 2: ATTACHING THE VERTEBRAL COLUMN TO THE WOODEN BASE

1. Hold the vertebral column over the top of the wooden base with the ends of the vertical supports touching the surface, making sure that the verticals *are* vertical. Move the vertebral column until it looks properly positioned in the middle of the wooden base. Mark the position of the vertical supports with a pencil. Alternately, if you have a sheet of Styrofoam, you can temporarily mount your partially completed dinosaur on this, by simply pushing the vertical supports through the material. This will give you the chance to check the distances between the verticals and will also allow you to experiment with the position of the skeleton, before marking the drill holes in the wooden base.

2. Make two holes in the base for the vertical supports. This can be done using the points of the nail scissors or, preferably, an electric drill (use a $\frac{5}{64}$-inch bit). The holes must not be any wider than the coat hanger, otherwise the vertical supports will not fit tightly into the base. The holes should be drilled to a depth that is about ⅛ inch (3 mm) less than that of the thickness of the board. If you are using an electric drill, this is best done by measuring off the required depth from the tip of the drill bit, and marking this with a piece of masking tape. Drill down into the wooden base until the masking tape marker just touches the surface.

3. Firmly grip the straight end of one of the vertical supports with the pliers, about ¾ inch (2 cm) from its end, and push it into the hole as far as it will go. It should be a tight fit, and the vertical support should be held firm. If it's loose, pull it out and make the hole deeper.

4. Check the distance between the top surface of the wooden base and the top of the vertical support. This has to be 9.5 cm. If it is less, ease the vertical support out of the hole a little. If the distance is greater, deepen the hole or, if need be, snip a little off the end of the vertical support.

5. Repeat steps 3 and 4 for the second vertical support.

## STEP 3: MOUNTING THE PELVIS

Before gluing the left and right halves of the pelvis to the backbone, you need to check that they fit together properly. Just to remind yourself which way round the two halves of the pelvis go, see the illustration on page 70.

Hold the right half of the pelvis in your left hand with the front end pointing toward you. Do the same for the left side in your right hand. Line up the two ilia so that they just touch—and so that their anterior ends are on the same level. The tips of the other two bones (the pubis in front and the ischium behind) should touch their opposite partners. If necessary, adjust the positions of the bones until they all line up. This is done by applying gentle pressure to the bones that need repositioning—there is enough resilience in the cement holding them together to allow them to move slightly. When you're satisfied that the two halves match up properly, do the following. You may want to get the help of a second pair of hands for this.

1. Cut off a 7-inch (18 cm) length of twist tie. Hold the two halves of the pelvis together in one hand, lined up as they were when you were checking them. Thread the twist tie through both hip sockets.
2. Keeping the twist tie straight for the moment, put the pelvis beneath the vertebral column, making sure that the front end faces toward the neck. Adjust the position of the two halves of the pelvis so that:

    1. The hip sockets are opposite the vertical support.
    2. The inside surfaces of the left and right ilia are touching the vertebrae.
    3. The top edges of the two ilia are only about 1/16 inch (2

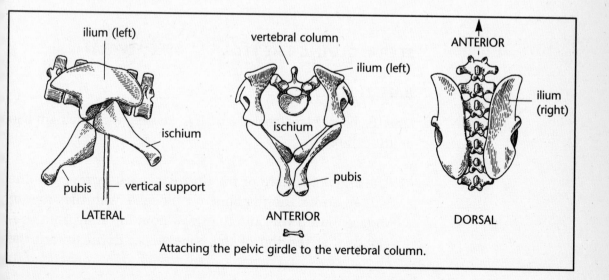

Attaching the pelvic girdle to the vertebral column.

mm) above the level of the tops of the neural spines of the sacral vertebrae.

4. The tips of the left and right pubes touch each other.

5. The tips of the left and right ischia touch each other, embracing the vertical support.

When you're sure that the pelvis is in the correct position, hold it in place with one hand and use the other hand to bend the ends of the twist tie upward. Bring the two ends together and twist them. Keep on twisting to take up the slack—this will hold the pelvis in the proper position. Gently let go of the pelvis, making sure that it does not move when you do so. If there is any movement, you can adjust the position of the pelvis by crimping the twist tie. You may find it useful to add a second loop of twist tie. Once the pelvis is fixed in its proper position, it is ready for gluing.

3. Using a toothpick, add beads of glue to all the points where the pelvis touches against the vertebral column. Use enough glue to make a good solid job of it.

While you're waiting for the glue to set (it'll take about half an hour), you can start gluing the lower parts of the back and front legs.

## STEP 4: GLUING THE LEGS

### *Back Legs*

Find the paper plate labeled *back legs*. Starting with the right leg, do the following:

1. The anterior surface of the tibia is marked by a pencil line and an arrow. Lay the bone on the table with the anterior surface toward you, and the arrow pointing away from you. Notice that the top of the bone slopes down toward the

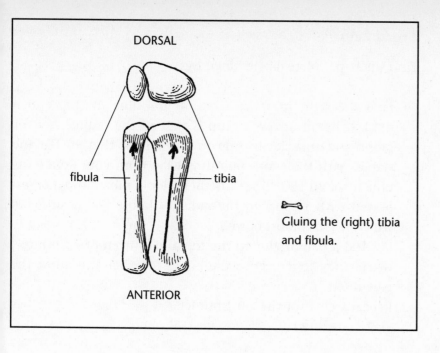

DORSAL

fibula —— tibia

ANTERIOR

Gluing the (right) tibia and fibula.

outer edge of the shaft, where there is a well-marked depression. The upper end of the inner edge of the shaft, in contrast, is convex.

2. While steadying the tibia flat against the table with one hand, hold the fibula with your other one. The flattened upper end of the fibula should be at right angles to the surface of the table. Press the two bones together so that the upper end of the fibula fits into the depression on the tibia. Does the fibula bow in or out from the shaft of the tibia? Rotate the axis of the fibula through 180° and check again. Choose the position in which the fibula bows in toward the tibia. Add beads of glue to the top and bottom contact edges of both bones. Allow them to dry for a minute or two, then press the two bones firmly together and hold them until they are united.

3. Repeat steps 1 and 2 for the left leg.

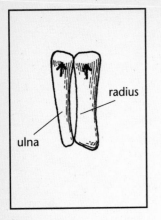

ulna  radius

Gluing the (right) radius and ulna.

### Front Legs

Find the paper plate labeled *front legs*.

1. Find the right front leg. Look at the ulna. Its top end is marked by an arrow; so too is that of the radius. Lay the radius and ulna side by side on the table, so they are flat and stable, with their tops pointing away from you. Rotate the ulna through 180° to see whether it looks more bowed or less bowed with respect to the radius. Choose the position in which it looks most bowed.

    Add a dab of glue to the top and bottom of each bone, where they touch. Press the bones together and allow the glue to set.

2. Repeat step 1 for the left front leg.

## STEP 5: MOUNTING THE RIBS

Check to make sure that the glue fixing the pelvis to the vertebrae has dried. If it hasn't, leave it to set for another half hour, then try again.

Gently try moving the pelvis to see that it is firmly attached. If in doubt, add more glue and leave for an hour to set.

When you are sure the pelvis is well and truly glued to the vertebrae, remove the twist tie and get ready to mount the ribs.

Cut two pieces of twist tie, each 10 inches (25 cm) long, and bend them into the shape shown in the illustration. Attach the ends of each twist tie to the vertical supports. These curved shapes are for supporting the ribs while they are being glued.

Find the plate labeled *ribs*. One set is labeled *right ribs*, the other *left ribs*. Start with the set of left ribs. Prop up the base of your dinosaur skeleton so that the right side leans toward the table and the left side faces you. Do the following:

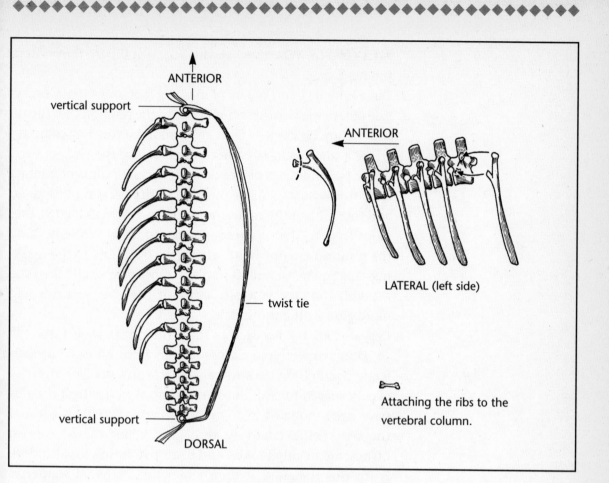

ANTERIOR

vertical support

ANTERIOR

twist tie

LATERAL (left side)

vertical support

DORSAL

Attaching the ribs to the vertebral column.

1. Look at the first rib. As you saw earlier, the ribs are forked with one branch shorter than the other. The short branch attaches to the transverse process of the vertebra, while the long branch attaches to a small depression in the side of the vertebra—take a look at the illustration on page 30 to remind yourself. Hold the rib up to the first dorsal vertebra (the one that is immediately behind the front vertical support) and try articulating its two branches. You may get a good fit, with the rib curving downward and backward. However, it may be necessary to use the nail clippers to snip about 2 mm off the end of the longest branch of the fork to

get a good fit. When you're satisfied with the fit, move on to the next step.

2. Cut a ½ inch (1 cm) square of masking tape and stick it, sticky-side out, to the twist-tie rib support, in the position that the rib will occupy. (Sticky side faces away from the vertebral column.)

3. Using a toothpick, put a bead of glue onto the ends of each of the two branches of the rib and on their points of contact with the vertebra. Allow the glue to dry for a minute or so and then attach the rib to the vertebra, as you did in the previous step, so that it curves down and back. While holding the rib steady in one hand, attach the other end to the masking-tape square to hold it in place. Once you've attached the rib with the tape you can let go. If need be, you can add more glue with a toothpick.

4. Repeat steps 1–3 for each of the other ribs in their turn.

Don't expect your dinosaur's ribs to be all lined up perfectly parallel to one another—they won't be! Nor are they evenly spaced in real dinosaur skeletons, not unless the ribs have been modeled in some other material. This is because the ribs, being relatively thin, and being curved in two planes, are readily broken and distorted during fossilization. Fossil ribs therefore seldom retain their original shape, so having uneven ribs in your skeleton will make it look all the more authentic.

5. Repeat steps 1–4 for the ribs of the right side.

Leave the ribs to dry for at least half an hour. While you're waiting, you can do the following jobs.

## STEP 6: FINAL GLUING OF THE LEGS

Find the paper plate labeled *back legs*.

1. Take the right femur and lay it flat on the table with the anterior surface facing toward you. Line up the glued right tibia and fibula beneath it, as shown in the illustration.

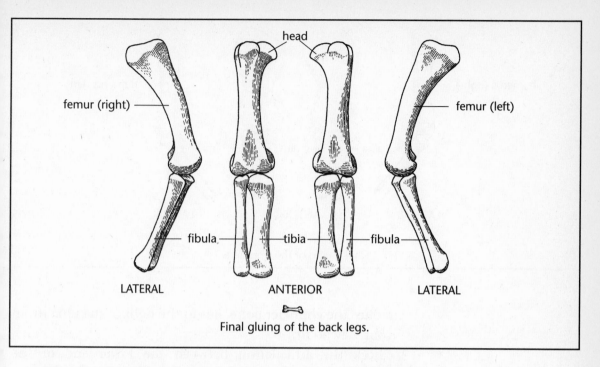

Final gluing of the back legs.

Make sure that the anterior side faces you (the upper end of the anterior surface of the tibia is hollowed). Also make sure that the fibula, the smaller of the two bones, is to the left of the tibia (from your viewpoint).

2. Check the articulation between the lower end of the femur and the upper end of the tibia and fibula. You may need to file a little from the top of the tibia to get a good fit. Add beads of glue to their contact surfaces, and allow them to dry for a minute or two. Press the articular surfaces together, angling the femur relative to the tibia and fibula, as shown in the illustration. Place them in a sandbox to set for about half an hour, with a label beside it that reads *right hind leg*.

3. Repeat steps 1 and 2 for the left hind leg.

Find the paper plate labeled *front legs*.

1. Take the right humerus and lay it flat on the table, with the anterior surface toward you. Lay the glued radius and ulna beneath it, as shown in the illustration. Make sure that the

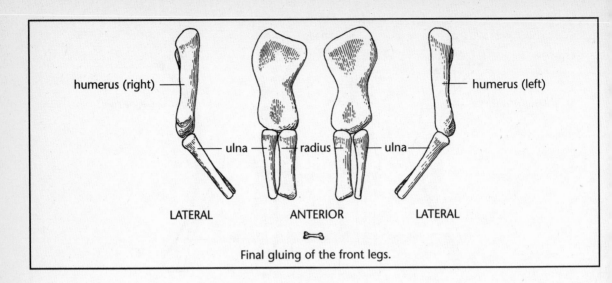

humerus (right)

ulna — radius — ulna

humerus (left)

LATERAL          ANTERIOR          LATERAL

Final gluing of the front legs.

radius, the chunkier bone, lies to the right of the ulna (from your viewpoint).

2. Check the articulation between the lower end of the humerus and the upper end of the radius and ulna. If necessary, adjust the contact by filing down the top of the radius or ulna. Add beads of glue to their contact surfaces, and allow them to dry for a minute or two. Press the articular surfaces together, angling the humerus relative to the radius and ulna as shown. Place these in a sandbox to set for about half an hour, with a label beside it that reads *right front leg*.

3. Repeat steps 1 and 2 for the left leg.

When the glue has dried and both pairs of legs are ready for mounting, clean off the pencil marks. Put the front legs and back legs back on their labeled paper plates.

## STEP 7: MOUNTING THE SKULL

1. Remove the floral tape from the front end of the backbone support. There should be about ½ inch (1 cm) of the bare

coat hanger projecting beyond the first neck vertebra. If there is more, carefully snip off the extra with the pliers, but only after the ribs have set.

2. Lower the skull in place so that it balances on the backbone support and looks like it does in the illustrated skeleton on page 101. If necessary, bend the end of the backbone support downward, using a pair of pliers and a narrow pair of forceps. Try positioning the skull again. When you've got a good fit, move on to the next step.

3. Take the skull off the backbone support and turn it upside down. Add a bead of glue just in front of the orbits. Add another bead of glue to the wire, about 6 mm in front of the first neck vertebra. Hold the upside-down skull close to the wire and blow on both beads of glue for about a minute to help them set.

4. Put the skull in place. Make sure it is level and that the back end of the skull just touches the front end of the first neck vertebra. If the skull won't stay in place, wrap a piece of floral tape around both it and the first vertebra. Be careful not to let any excess glue drip down onto the wooden base.

## STEP 8: MOUNTING THE SHOULDERS

Make sure the glue holding the ribs is set and that all the ribs are firmly in place. Carefully undo the masking tape used to steady them and remove the two twist ties to which the ribs were attached. You're now ready to attach the shoulders. Find the paper plate labeled *shoulder*.

1. Prop up the base of your dinosaur, as you did when gluing the ribs, with the left side of the skeleton facing you.

2. Find the left scapula (with its attached coracoid) and lay it at an angle across the first four ribs, as shown in the illustration. Arrange the scapula so that its top end is about ³⁄₁₆ inch

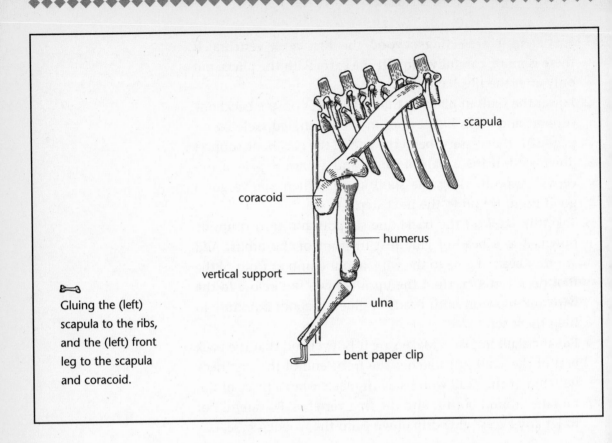

scapula

coracoid

humerus

vertical support

ulna

bent paper clip

**Gluing the (left) scapula to the ribs, and the (left) front leg to the scapula and coracoid.**

(5 mm) below the neural spines of the dorsal vertebrae. The anterior end of the coracoid should be level with the front vertical support.

3. Make a note of the approximate places of contact between the ribs and the scapula. Remove the scapula, apply dabs of glue to the contact areas, and allow to dry for a minute or so.

4. Return the scapula to the ribs, make any final adjustments, then allow the glue to dry. Using a toothpick, apply beads of glue to the contact areas between the scapula and the ribs, and allow these to dry for at least half an hour.

Repeat steps 1–4 for the right side of the dinosaur.

When both shoulders have set, stand your dinosaur skeleton upright again.

## STEP 9: MOUNTING THE LEGS

1. Open a paper clip and snip off and save the smaller loop, using pliers. Use the pliers to bend the last 5 mm of the loop into a right angle. Repeat this with three more paper clips.
2. Check to make sure that the glue attaching the shoulders to the ribs has dried.
3. Take the left front leg and hold it in its proper position, with the top of the humerus tucked in beneath the lower end of the scapula, as shown in the illustration. Adjust it until its pose looks realistic.

    Position one of the angled paper clips so that the loop rests on the wooden base, with the two prongs touching the back end of the lower part of the leg, as shown in the illustration. Making sure not to move the angled paper clip, remove the leg. Add a bead of cement (or Krazy Glue) to the paper clip loop to attach it to the base, and allow it to set.
4. Repeat step 3 for the right front leg.

You've now got to do the same thing for the back legs.

1. Take the left back leg and hold it in its proper position with the head of the femur resting against the socket in the pelvis. Position one of the angled paper clips as before, so that the loop rests on the wooden base with the two prongs touching the back end of the lower part of the leg. Remove the leg, making sure you don't move the angled paper clip. Add a bead of glue to the paper clip loop and allow it to set, thereby attaching it to the base.
2. Repeat step 1 for the right back leg.

When the angled paper clips have set, you're ready to glue the legs into position. **Important:** If you used Krazy Glue to cement the paper clips in place, make absolutely sure there are no sticky residues before proceeding with the next step. If the

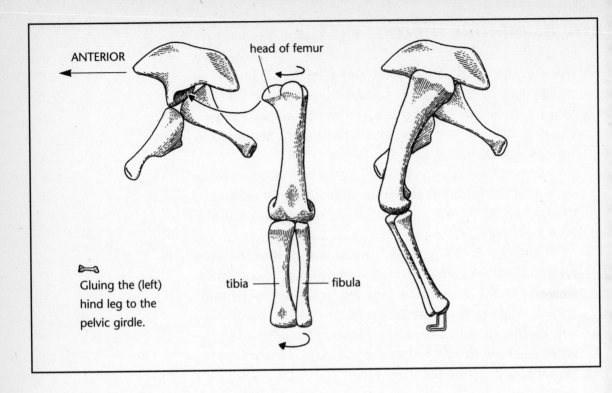

ANTERIOR

head of femur

tibia ——— ——— fibula

Gluing the (left) hind leg to the pelvic girdle.

glue is still sticky, it will bond with the plasticine that you are about to use.

Proceed as follows:

1. Make four small balls of plasticine, each with a diameter of about ¼ inch (6 mm). Press each one onto the loop part of the angled paper clip.
2. Take each leg in turn, as you did before, and hold it in its proper position. When you're satisfied with this position, remove the leg. Apply beads of glue to the points of contact between the top of the upper leg bone and the shoulder or pelvis. Allow a minute or so for the glue to dry. Then stick the upper leg bone into its proper position, pushing the lower end of the leg into the plasticine ball to help hold it all in place. Make any final adjustments in the positioning of the leg, then apply additional beads of glue to the places

where the leg contacts the rest of the skeleton. Small gaps between bones (up to about 3 mm) can be bridged with threads of glue. These can be added to later, when they have dried.

3. When the glue has set—about half an hour later—remove the plasticine ball. This should lift off cleanly, but any adherent scraps can be scraped off with a toothpick.

You now have to check the spacing between the bottom of each leg and the surface of the wooden board, to make sure each of the feet will fit in place properly. Proceed as follows:

1. Locate the right forefoot. You will see that it is flat where it has been lying on a flat surface, but it needs to be curved. Do this by bending the foot around the tip of one of your fingers, such that the outer toes (digits 1 and 5) are brought closer together. Try positioning the foot beneath the end of the right front leg. The digits need to be almost vertical. If there is not enough space to accommodate the foot, increase the gap by carefully raising the front vertical support from its hole in the wooden board. Do this by firmly gripping the lowermost end of the vertical support with downward-angled pliers, placing something solid beneath them for leverage. Gently push down on the handle-end of the pliers to ease the vertical support a few millimeters from its hole. Check the distance again by holding the foot in position, adjusting the gap as necessary.
2. Repeat step 1 for the left front foot.
3. Repeat steps 1 and 2 for the hind legs and feet, but incline the digits at about 45° rather than making them almost vertical.

When satisfied with the spacing between the ends of the legs and the wooden board, the lower ends of the legs can be glued. Using a toothpick, apply beads of glue to the bottom of the lower leg, extending this onto the front of the paper clip support. Allow the glue to dry, adding more if necessary. Since the foot will cover the paper clip, this additional glue will not show.

## STEP 10: MOUNTING THE FEET

This last step is easy! Find the front and back feet and proceed as follows:

1.  Using a toothpick, apply a thread of glue to the front edge of the bottom of the right front leg. Apply a thread of glue to the top edge of the corresponding foot. Wait for a minute or so, then attach the foot to the bottom of the leg. If necessary, an additional thread of glue can be added to the contact zone.
2. Repeat step 1 for the other legs.

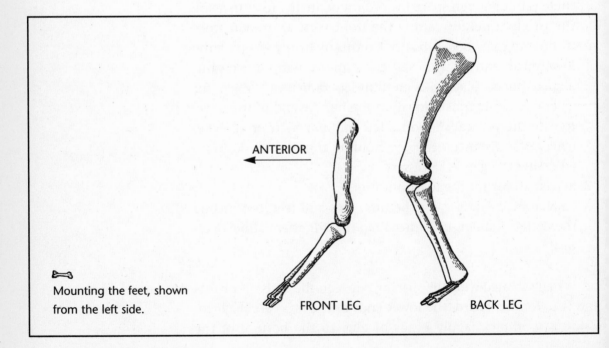

Mounting the feet, shown from the left side.

ANTERIOR

FRONT LEG     BACK LEG

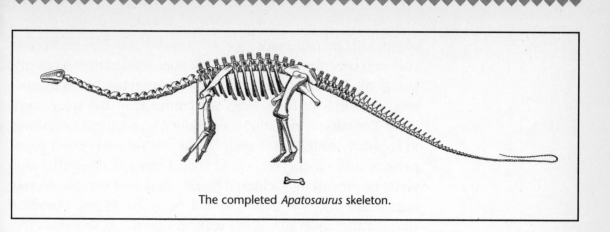

The completed *Apatosaurus* skeleton.

Congratulations! You've now got your very own dinosaur skeleton.

## AN ADDED TOUCH

Dinosaurs, like other reptiles, have small Y-shaped bones attached to the bottoms of many of their caudal vertebrae. These bones are called **chevrons**. Chevron bones are absent from the most anterior caudal vertebrae, and do not continue to the tip

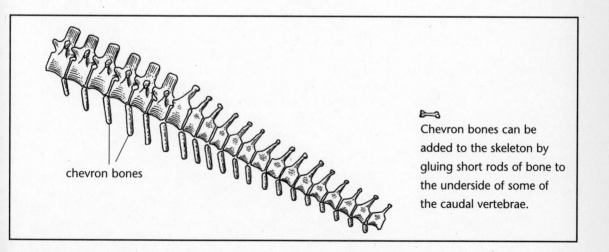

chevron bones

Chevron bones can be added to the skeleton by gluing short rods of bone to the underside of some of the caudal vertebrae.

of the tail. In sauropods like *Apatosaurus* and *Diplodocus*, the chevrons become horizontal rods of bone toward the end of the tail. If you wish, you can make 20 or so chevron bones by cutting some rods of bone from the remnants in the spare parts plate. The largest ones should be about 8 mm long, diminishing in length to only 3 or 4 mm. If you don't have enough spare parts to make them, you could collect some more sternal and vertebral ribs from a chicken-breast meal and use these. The improvised chevron bones should be glued to the posterior edges of the underside of the vertebral centra, as shown in the illustration, and should point down and back.

# PART 3
# WHAT SORT OF DINOSAUR?

**B**rontosaurus, as many of us know, is not a proper name—the official name for the dinosaur you've built is *Apatosaurus*. It is by no means unusual for more than one scientific name to have been given to a particular animal, but to understand how this happens requires some explanation of the way animals are named. Scientific names for animals comprise two parts: The first, which starts with a capital letter, is the generic name, while the second, which always starts with a lowercase letter, is referred to as the specific name. The lion, for example, is *Panthera leo*, while its relative the mountain lion is *Panthera concolor*. When a new animal is discovered, the first person who publishes its description is entitled to name it, provided he or she follows certain rules, as set out in *The International Code of Zoological Nomenclature*. Basically, there has to be a specimen, called the type specimen or holotype, upon which the name of the species is founded. The description has to be sufficiently detailed that the specimen can be recognized, and this should include an illustration. Comparisons also have to be made with similar species to show that the new species is sufficiently different to warrant its erection. Once an adequate description of a new species has been published, the new name is official, and no other name can subsequently be applied to that species.

Othniel Charles Marsh (1831–1899), one of North America's pioneer dinosaur specialists, erected the name *Brontosaurus* in 1879, based on two large skeletons found at Como Bluff, Wyoming, the same year. Gigantic dinosaurs like these, characterized by their long necks, long tails, and **quadrupedal** (four-footed) posture, are collectively called sauropods, as we saw earlier. Marsh designated the best of his two skeletons—still one of the most complete sauropods ever found—as the holotype of a new species, *Brontosaurus excelsus*. Two years later, he designated the second skeleton as the holotype of *Brontosaurus amplus*.

Marsh published an illustration of the skeleton of *Brontosaurus excelsus* in 1883, giving the world its first glimpse of what these gigantic creatures may have looked like. This was the first time anyone had ever illustrated the skeleton of a sauropod dinosaur, and it placed the name *Brontosaurus*—and its archetypal image embodying everything dinosaurian—firmly in the public consciousness.

The skeleton itself was eventually put on public display at Yale University's Peabody Museum, where it remains today, but this was not the first time a sauropod skeleton had ever been exhibited. That honor goes to yet another skeleton of the same dinosaur, which went on display at the American Museum of Natural History in 1905. By that time, however, an ugly truth had been discovered about *Brontosaurus*.

Two years before erecting the name *Brontosaurus*, Marsh had described a different sauropod genus, which he named *Apatosaurus*. *Apatosaurus* was based upon a sacrum and some vertebrae (more of the specimen was found later, and Marsh's collectors eventually excavated most of the skeleton). However, when paleontologist E. S. Riggs made some comparisons between this material and the two skeletons that Marsh had used to establish *Brontosaurus*, he found no significant differences between them. All of the material belonged to the same genus, and, since the name *Apatosaurus* was the oldest, it had priority. The name *Brontosaurus* was therefore rejected (it is referred to as a junior synonym). Although it is almost a century since Riggs dismissed the name *Brontosaurus*, it still gets used from time to time. Fairly recently, for example, the United States Postal Service introduced a series of dinosaur stamps, one of which depicted *Apatosaurus*, inappropriately named *Brontosaurus*. Notwithstanding Stephen Jay Gould's spirited defense of *Brontosaurus* in his book *Bully for Brontosaurus*, it is a dead name among paleontologists and should be allowed to rest in peace.

The discrepancy over names is not the only confusion associated with the magnificent skeleton that Marsh described and illustrated. Although the skeleton is one of the most complete sauropods ever found, several parts were missing, including the skull (it is rare to find a complete dinosaur skeleton). Marsh

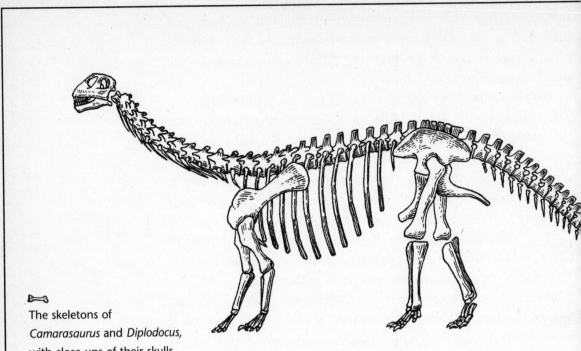

The skeletons of *Camarasaurus* and *Diplodocus,* with close-ups of their skulls.

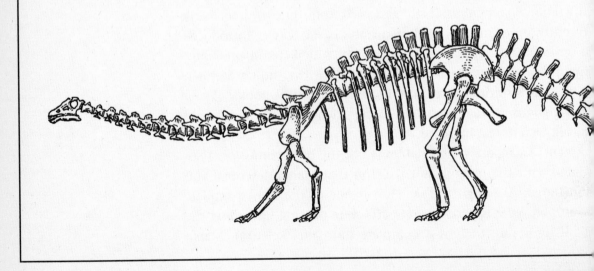

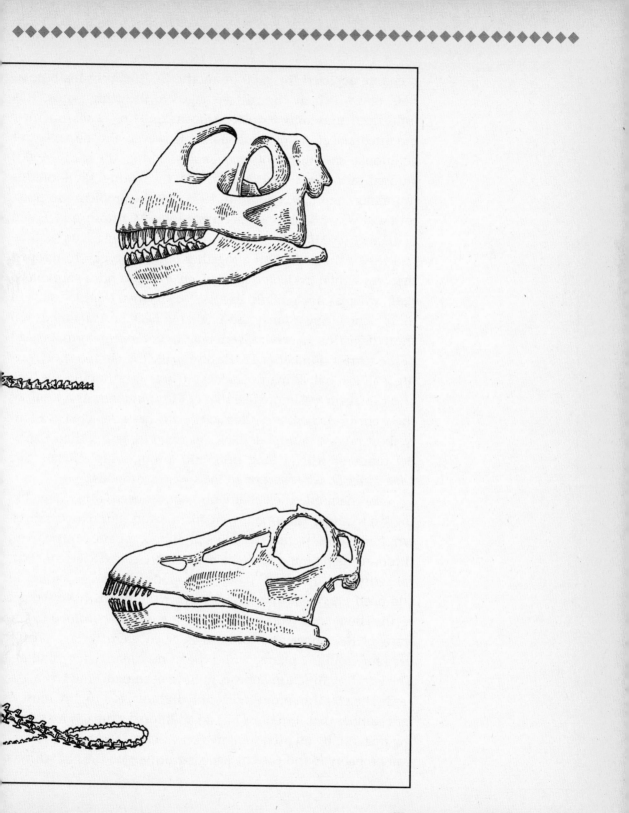

therefore depicted the skull of another specimen in his restoration, one which he thought belonged to the same genus. This influenced museums to place similar kinds of skulls on their mounted skeletons of *Apatosaurus*. However, the discovery of additional specimens of *Apatosaurus* during the early 1900s aroused suspicions that Marsh had the wrong skull on his restoration. But it was not until 1975 that the problem was finally resolved, by sauropod specialists John McIntosh and David Berman. They showed that Marsh had been wrong. The skull he had used belonged to an altogether different type of sauropod that was similar to *Camarasaurus*. *Camarasaurus* has a short, deep skull, whereas *Apatosaurus,* like its close relative *Diplodocus,* has a more slender one. Marsh also made the neck of *Apatosaurus* too short, depicting 12 cervical vertebrae, as in *Camarasaurus,* instead of the correct number of 15. He also made the tail too short, giving it almost half as many caudal vertebrae as it should have had, and this again was more like that of *Camarasaurus*. As a result of these errors, *Apatosaurus* has traditionally been depicted as a fairly short, robust sauropod, like *Camarasaurus,* rather than a slender dinosaur with a long neck and a long whiplash tail, like *Diplodocus*. So what sort of animals were sauropods?

Like the modern elephant, and almost every other large living land animal, sauropods were plant eaters. But whereas modern herbivores—zebra, wildebeest, hippo, giraffe, bison, and rhino, to name but a few—have an impressive battery of teeth for grinding up their food, sauropods appear woefully ill equipped. *Apatosaurus* and many other sauropods have slender teeth. These are few in number and are mostly confined to the front of the upper and lower jaws. Such teeth were probably used for cropping plants, with little or no capacity for grinding. The grinding function appears to have been performed by a gizzard. The gizzard, found today only in birds, is a highly muscular chamber that functions like an additional stomach for grinding up food. If you used supermarket chickens for your dinosaur, you probably found the chicken's gizzard inside the bag with its neck and liver. It is about the size of a small walnut and has thick muscular walls. Its grinding action is assisted by gizzard stones—small stones that birds swallow from time to time to replace those that are lost. Incidentally, this is why chickens, and many other birds, need a source of grit or gravel. We believe that sauropods had gizzards because smoothly polished stones, reminiscent of gizzard stones, have been found in the stomach regions of some sauropod skeletons. Perhaps other dinosaurs, like their avian (bird) kin, also had gizzards.

Previous generations of paleontologists pictured sauropods as slothful behemoths, often showing them as living in water because they were believed to have been too massive to support their weight on dry land. Recently, however, it has become fashionable to give sauropods the cut and dash of spring lambs. Contemporary artists and filmmakers alike, no doubt influenced by avant-garde paleontologist Robert Bakker, show them gamboling along at great speed, and even rearing up on their hind legs to defend themselves from predators. Somewhere between these two extremes is where the truth likely lies.

It is not my intention to give a detailed treatment of sauropods here because this information is available elsewhere (see Further Reading). Instead, I offer an overview of some of the problems faced by living giants, drawing some inferences for sauropods from these. I will also consider some of the adaptations that sauropods evolved for supporting their massive bodies.

The largest land animal living today is the African elephant, which weighs up to about 6 tons. If you watch elephants at the zoo, you soon get some idea of what it must be like carrying so much weight about. Their actions are slow and deliberate, whether they are ambling along or stopping to pick something up with their trunks. They walk with their legs held straight, a strategy for reducing the stresses on their limb bones. They also maintain a similar stiff-legged posture when running, giving them an awkward, ungainly gait. That they can still outrun us, despite this, is attributable to their large size—just consider how long their strides are relative to ours. Compared with most other large tetrapods, elephants are slow runners, with a top speed of about 22 mph (35 km/h) compared with 43 mph (70 km/h) for zebra, 50 mph (80 km/h) for wildebeest, and 37 mph (60 km/h) for lion. Unlike other tetrapods, elephants are unable to gallop, because this would place undue stresses on their bones. Sometimes they raise themselves up on their hind legs to reach up higher into trees with their trunks, but they do this slowly and deliberately, thereby avoiding putting too much stress on their bones. Avoiding undue stress is very important to them, and they take particular care when moving over uncertain terrain, to reduce the chances of stumbling. If an elephant did take a tumble, the injuries sustained could be fatal. Elephants even have problems when lying down, and are unable to doze for more than about an hour at a time because of the compressive damage to the side in contact with the ground. Nerves can be injured, muscles bruised, and blood clots formed in the blood vessels, the latter of which can be fatal.

Another consequence of the elephant's large size is that it has a relatively small surface area for its volume. Like other mammals (and birds), they are warm-blooded, and most of their excess body heat is lost through the skin. Since their skin surface is relatively small, they have difficulty shedding this excess heat and are consequently prone to heat stroke. The reverse holds true in the cold—they conserve body heat—which explains why captive elephants are able to tolerate North American winters.

As we saw earlier, elephants stand and walk with the soles and palms of their feet raised off the ground, cushioned by an extensive rubbery pad. If you watch an elephant at the zoo, you will see how the pad balloons out when the foot is lifted from the ground. When the pad touches the ground again it flattens out and spreads, reminiscent of an underinflated tire. The pad is remarkably resilient, like dense foam rubber.

The front feet are larger than the hind ones because they carry more weight. The extra weight is due to the massive head, which weighs about a ton in adult males. Keeping the head up takes a lot of effort, and several anatomical features help in this. The most striking feature is the extreme shortness of the neck, which reduces the leverage exerted on the skeleton. Like all other mammals (giraffes too!), the elephant has seven cervical vertebrae, but these are quite short, being flattened from front to back. The neural spines of the vertebrae in the shoulder region are tall and robust, providing a substantial anchorage for the muscles and ligaments that attach to the back of the head. The largest of these ligaments is called the **nuchal ligament**. The nuchal ligament is an important part of the head-supporting mechanism of tetrapods, especially those with large heads. Unlike other ligaments in the body, which have little pliancy, the nuchal ligament is as resilient as rubber. When the head is depressed, the nuchal ligament stretches like a rubber band, and this helps raise the head again, thereby saving muscle energy. Since the elephant's neck is so short, it is unable to reach the ground with its head. Even if it could do so, its tusks would prevent it from picking up food; therefore, the elephant relies on its trunk for feeding.

The tallest animal living today is the giraffe, which reaches a height of up to 16 feet (5 m). Having its head placed some 10 feet (3 m) above its heart presents some interesting blood pressure problems. First, the pressure of the blood leaving the heart has to be high enough to drive it all the way up the neck to the head. But the blood has to be at a sufficiently high pressure when it reaches the head to force it through the fine network of blood vessels in the brain and other organs. To achieve this, the blood leaves the heart at a pressure that is probably the highest of any living mammal, and about twice as high as our own. The pressure is so high that it would probably rupture the blood vessels of any other animal, but two mechanisms prevent this. First, the walls of a giraffe's **arteries** are much thicker than in other mammals (arteries carry blood away from the heart). Second, the giraffe has a thick and tightly fitting hide that functions like the pressure suits worn by jet fighter pilots.

The unpleasant dizzy sensation we sometimes experience when standing quickly from a prone position is caused by a temporary fall in the pressure of the blood reaching our brain. Giraffes sometimes lie down to rest, and when they stand up they have to do so in stages, first squatting and waiting for a few moments before standing fully erect. This presumably allows the vascular system to stabilize. If a giraffe suddenly raised its head to its full height, it would probably become faint. Conversely, when a giraffe is browsing or drinking, its head is lower than its heart, and the blood pressure is accordingly higher. But the fine blood vessels of the head are protected from the pressure increase by the constriction of the vessels supplying them with blood.

Humans are not very tall, yet the height difference between our lower legs and heart is enough to cause a problem in returning blood to the heart. This is primarily because blood in the **veins**—the vessels that return blood to the heart—flows at such low pressures. This is because of the way the circulatory system works. The high-pressure blood leaving the heart in the arteries has to be distributed to all parts of the body. The blood is forced through progressively smaller vessels, from arteries to **arterioles**, and then through the extensive network of **capillaries**—the smallest vessels—that supply various tissues with blood. Because of the resistance offered to its passage, the blood leaves the capillaries at a low pressure. From here it passes into **venules**, then finally into the veins. The blood from the legs now has to flow against gravity to make its way back to the heart. The pumping action of the leg muscles, by pressing against the veins, greatly assists the return flow. This is because veins have valves, which allow blood to flow only toward the heart. Consequently, when the leg muscles massage the veins, blood is squeezed toward the heart. The extreme discomfort experienced by soldiers when standing still on a parade ground is mainly because their leg muscles are inactive. The muscles are therefore not helping to pump blood back to the heart. The resulting reduction in blood return to the heart can lower the blood pressure to the head, causing the soldier to faint.

The problem of returning blood to a giraffe's heart is even more acute than in a human because its legs are so much longer. The tightly fitting hide covering the legs appears to reduce the extent of blood pooling and so too does the giraffe's ability to restrict the flow of blood to the capillaries of the legs. The pumping action of the leg muscles may be a significant factor too, but we still have much to learn about the giraffe's circulatory system.

Sauropods were considerably heavier than elephants and they had longer necks than giraffes, so their potential problems were manifestly greater. Does this mean that the conservative interpretation of the early paleontologists, who visualized sauropods as slothful monsters, incapable of supporting their massive bodies on dry land, was closest to the truth?

The idea that sauropods were too heavy to support their weight on dry land was abandoned a long time ago, primarily on the evidence of trackways. Sauropod trackways, characterized by the large round imprints of their elephantine feet, were discovered in 1938 by Roland Bird, a paleontologist with the American Museum of Natural History. These particular trackways, found in Texas, had been made by a sauropod like *Apatosaurus,* and revealed a great deal about the animals that made them. The hind prints are larger than the fore prints, corresponding to the differences in size of their respective foot skeletons. They are also more deeply imprinted, showing that most of the body weight was borne by the hind limbs. This agrees with the fact that the hind legs are more massive than the forelegs. It is also supported by independent evidence that the **center of mass** (the balance point of the body) was close to the pelvis. If the track-makers had been walking along buoyed up by water, it is unlikely there would have been a difference in depth between the fore- and hind legs. Furthermore, some of the prints had scrolls of mud preserved, where the soft terrain had been squeezed out at the sides of the feet. If the animals had been walking in water, this mud would have been swirled away.

*Apatosaurus*, by no means the heaviest of sauropods, reached lengths of about 75 feet (23 m) and an estimated weight of 28 tons. That's about five times heavier than an elephant, so we can be fairly confident that their lifestyle would have been at least as unhurried as the elephant's. Carrying such an enormous weight would have placed a great burden on the skeleton, which had several mechanical strategies for dealing with the problem. The limb bones, like those of the elephant, were kept essentially vertical, as evidenced by the placement of their articular surfaces at the very ends of the bones. The limb bones were also solid, like an elephant's, maximizing their ability to withstand the compressive forces bearing down on them.

The individual vertebrae are massive, especially the dorsal ones, whose centra are about 1 foot (35 cm) in diameter. As a weight-reducing strategy, bone is concentrated in regions sub-

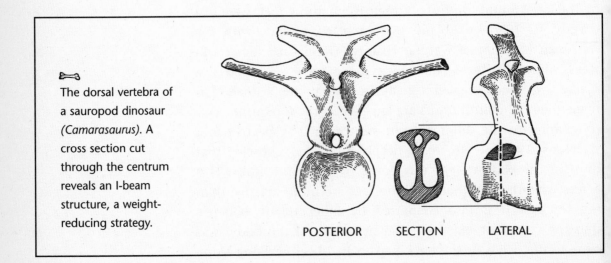

The dorsal vertebra of a sauropod dinosaur *(Camarasaurus)*. A cross section cut through the centrum reveals an I-beam structure, a weight-reducing strategy.

POSTERIOR          SECTION          LATERAL

jected to the highest stresses, bony struts and flanges replacing solid bone. To this end, each centrum has a deep excavation on either side. If you cut a slice through one of these vertebrae and looked at it head-on, you would see that it had the shape of an engineer's I-beam. The I-beam is a device that gives maximum strength for minimum weight, which is precisely the strategy in the sauropods' vertebrae.

Most of the dorsal and cervical vertebrae articulate together by a well-developed ball-and-socket joint between adjacent centra. This would have added to the load-bearing capacity of the vertebral column. The neural spines are tall, especially in the dorsal and anterior caudal vertebrae. This provided a long leverage—and also a large attachment area—for the ligaments and muscles that moved and maintained the shape of the vertebral column. Some sauropods, including *Apatosaurus,* have prominently forked neural spines in the neck and shoulder regions, and these probably served as a guide for an extensive nuchal ligament.

I recently visited Berlin to examine the skeleton of *Brachiosaurus,* one of the heaviest of sauropods (estimated weight 78 tons). The feature that most impressed me, besides its unbelievable size, was the delicacy of its cervical vertebrae. The

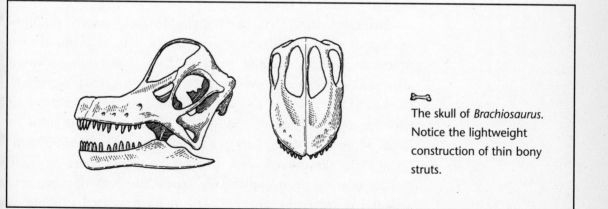

The skull of *Brachiosaurus.* Notice the lightweight construction of thin bony struts.

largest of these was almost 3 feet long (1 m), but it was very lightly built, with thin bony struts and webs of bone that were almost paper-thin. Another strategy for reducing the load borne by the neck is to have a small and lightly built skull, a feature of all sauropods. The skull of *Brachiosaurus* is about as large as that of a horse, but it is so lightly constructed that it would have weighed considerably less than a horse's skull.

Measurements taken from a mounted skeleton of *Apatosaurus,* where the neck is essentially horizontal, give a value of almost 7 feet (2 m) for the vertical distance between the head and heart. This means that the animal's blood pressure would need to have been almost twice as high as ours, just to supply the head with blood. Of course, if it had raised its neck, the pressure requirement would have been considerably higher. And if sauropods had stood on their hind legs to reach higher into the trees, as Bakker proposed, the pressure differential would have been higher still. Similar measurements taken from the mounted skeleton of *Brachiosaurus* give a value of 22 feet (6.5 m) for the distance between head and heart. This would have required a blood pressure about twice as high as that of the giraffe's, just to supply the head. Several ad hoc proposals have been made to explain how sauropods may have overcome these seemingly insurmountable circulatory problems, but I remain unconvinced. The most fanciful of these is that sauropods had ancillary hearts in their necks.

Little attention has been given to how much mobility sauropods may have had in their necks. This is primarily for practical reasons, because most of the continuous series of sauropod vertebrae are permanently joined together in mounted skeletons. However, English paleontologist John Martin had the rare opportunity of examining a well-preserved neck in detail while assembling part of a skeleton of *Cetiosaurus* for exhibition. He discovered that neck movements were severely restricted in the vertical plane, because of the way the vertebrae articulated with one another. The head appeared capable of reaching the ground, but the neck could not be raised more than about 30° above the horizontal. Perhaps this is how sauropods resolved their potential blood pressure problems: by restricting vertical head movements and using their long necks mainly for making wide horizontal sweeps.

Contrary to the assertions of some paleontologists, who would have us believe we know everything about dinosaurs—from their breeding behavior and body temperatures to how fast they ran—we will never know what dinosaurs were *really* like. All we can do is make deductions and educated guesses, based on what we know of the dinosaurs' earthly remains and of living animals.

It seems very doubtful to me that sauropods, or many other dinosaurs, were warm-blooded, in the same way that modern mammals and birds are. Birds and mammals achieve their high, and generally constant, body temperatures by virtue of their high metabolic rates, but this is very expensive in terms of food requirements. For example, a lioness consumes about 20 times her body mass in a year, compared with about four times its body mass for a 6-foot-long (1.7 m) Komodo lizard, a cold-blooded animal. Given that an elephant spends about 75 percent of its time feeding, day and night, it is difficult to see how a sauropod, weighing five times more, could have obtained enough food if it had a mammalian level of metabolism. And how would such a sauropod have gotten rid of excess heat, given the heat dissipation problems of elephants?

It also seems doubtful that sauropods would have been very active animals. Elephants, we have seen—mere lightweights in comparison—live very unhurried lives. I have a vivid imagination, but I cannot envision a sauropod dashing along, the way they are depicted by so many modern artists. Nor can I conceive of their rearing up on their hind legs, whether to feed on tall trees or fend off attackers. I picture sauropods as rather sedate creatures, ambling along gently when need be, and letting their necks "do the walking" wherever possible, sweeping their heads from side to side in great arcs as they browsed on the foliage. I also imagine they were much more slender than they are often depicted—more like greyhounds than hippos. And their tranquil lives, in that far-off Mesozoic world, may have lasted for more than a century.

A reconstruction of *Apatosaurus*.

# CONTENTS OF THE LABELED PLATES

◆◆◆◆◆◆◆◆◆◆◆◆

What the individual bones will become is given in parentheses unless they retain their original identities.

| PLATE NAME | CONTENTS |
|---|---|
| Ribs | One set of forked ribs, size-ordered. |
| Vertebrae | At least 3 groups of vertebrae from each chicken, labeled *neck and back vertebrae, sacral vertebrae,* and *tail vertebrae.* Home-cooked birds will also have an anterior neck-vertebrae string attached to the neck-and-back-vertebrae string. Also three furculae and four fibulae (terminal caudal vertebrae). |
| Skull | Three sterna (skull and mandibles). |
| Shoulder | One pair of scapulae and one pair of sternal bones (coracoids). |
| Pelvis | One pair of ilia and two pairs of ischia. One pair of ischia become the dinosaur's pubes. |

| PLATE NAME | CONTENTS |
|---|---|
| Back legs and feet | One pair of femora, one pair of hand bones (fibulae), one pair of ulnae (tibiae—singular, tibia), ten straight sternal ribs (foot and toe bones). |
| Front legs and feet | One pair of humeri, one pair of hand bones (radii), one pair of radii (ulnae), ten straight sternal ribs, and one fibula (foot and toe bones).[1] |

---

[1]The backbone string is the length of twist tie upon which the dinosaur's vertebrae are collected.

# RECIPES

◆◆◆◆◆◆◆◆◆◆◆

If you boil a whole chicken you will obtain about one pint of stock and 2–3 pounds of meat. As I'm concerned about minimizing fat intake, I always skin chickens before cooking them, removing most of the fat that lies beneath the skin, too. The skin should be saved and frozen for making stock.

## ANDY FORESTER'S FAMOUS GARLIC SOUP

With apologies to my good friend Andy for any transgression from the true path to garlic soup heaven.

*Makes two generous servings. Preparation time about 15 minutes, cooking time about 25 minutes.*

5 bulbs of garlic
1 pint of chicken stock
Salt, to taste
About 1 tablespoon of olive oil

1.  In choosing your garlic, be very selective. Garlic must be fresh and firm. Separate the individual cloves. Cut the ends off each clove and remove the husk. It may be easier to remove the husk if you first split the clove by laying the flat of a knife against it, and banging the knife with your hand. Andy never bothers husking the garlic because he sieves the soup prior to serving, but I find sieving to be a time-consuming bother.
2.  Heat the chicken stock on a low burner, almost to boiling. Meanwhile, sauté the peeled cloves over low heat, turning fre-

quently. Take great care not to let them burn. Cook until golden brown. Strain off any excess oil, and then transfer the sautéed garlic to a blender.

3. When the stock is ready, add it to the sautéed garlic, almost filling the blender, and turn it to its highest setting for about one minute.

4. Transfer contents of blender to an empty saucepan and stir in the rest of the chicken stock. (If you like your soup really thick, you may not want to add all of the rest of the stock.) Heat to serving temperature. Enjoy.

# WHAT TO DO WITH BOILED CHICKEN MEAT

You can use the chicken meat in any of your favorite recipes that call for chicken, such as stir-fries, curries, and salads. I offer the following for a quick and simple meal.

## CHICKEN-STUFFED SQUASH

*Serves four. Preparation time about five minutes, cooking time about 30 minutes.*

    Meat from one chicken
    2 small acorn squash
    1 cup of plum sauce or sweet mustard, according to taste
    1 tablespoon of sunflower seeds

1. Halve the squash and scoop out the pulp. Place the squash halves, cut edges down, onto a baking sheet and bake for about 30 minutes in a preheated oven set to 400° F (200° C). (Alternately, bake in a microwave set on high for about 20 minutes.) Check progress during baking by squeezing with an oven-mitted hand—if the squash is still firm, continue cooking.

2. Combine plum sauce and chicken in a saucepan and simmer for several minutes, stirring continuously.
3. Remove baked squash halves from the oven and allow them to cool for five minutes.
4. Remove the saucepan from the stove and allow it to cool for a minute or so. Stir in the sunflower seeds and spoon contents into the squash halves.

## MCGOWAN'S HONEYED CHICKEN

*Serves 3–4. Preparation time about ten minutes, cooking time approximately 1 hour and 20 minutes.*

> 1 chicken, skinned
> 1–2 tablespoons of honey
> approximately 1 teaspoon of ground ginger

Preheat oven to 350° F (175° C). Place the skinned bird, breast down, in an oven dish or pan that has been thoroughly sprayed with oil.

Heat the honey to boiling point, either in a small saucepan or in the microwave. Using a pastry brush (or a spoon), liberally paint the bird with hot honey, then sprinkle generously with ground ginger. Turn the bird breast up and repeat process. Place bird in the oven.

After half an hour of baking, remove chicken from oven and baste the bird with juice from the pan. This will ensure that the bird is good and brown. Cover chicken with a tent of aluminum foil and return it to the oven for another 50 minutes. Check bird at the end of this time. If not well browned, remove foil, baste, and bake for another five minutes.

Remove bird from pan and pour stock into a glass or separator to settle. Separate and discard top layer of oil. If the stock is thick, dilute it with a little water. Heat stock in a saucepan. Carve the bird, moistening the white meat with the stock. Any additional stock can be used as a sauce.

# FIFTY FABULOUS DISCUSSION TOPICS

◆◆◆◆◆◆◆◆◆◆◆◆

1. What is so interesting about the timing of the discovery of *Archaeopteryx*?
2. What features does *Archaeopteryx* share with dinosaurs such as *Tyrannosaurus*?
3. How does *Archaeopteryx* differ from dinosaurs like *Tyrannosaurus*?
4. Name some theropod dinosaurs.
5. List some features that theropods share.
6. Do you think chickens and their feathered relatives should be called birds or dinosaurs?
7. To what group of dinosaurs does *Apatosaurus* belong?
8. If birds are dinosaurs, why doesn't the skeleton of a chicken look more like that of *Tyrannosaurus*?
9. Give three features that birds share with other theropods.
10. What is the function of the spinal cord?
11. What was the basis for the incorrect idea that some dinosaurs, like *Stegosaurus*, had two brains?
12. Why does the spinal cord of humans, and other tetrapods, have a sacral swelling, and another enlargement in the shoulder region?
13. When building your dinosaur, why is it necessary to shorten the chicken's ilium?
14. Why can't the chicken's coracoid be used for your dinosaur's coracoid?

15. Why can't the chicken's pubis be used for your dinosaur's pubis?
16. Why does the chicken's femur have to be shortened to make it into your dinosaur's femur?
17. How would you know whether the chicken you were served in a restaurant was young or old?
18. What is a bird's alula? How can we get to see it being used?
19. Name some sauropod dinosaurs, and list some of their characteristics.
20. Name the major bones in the body.
21. Where are red blood cells formed in the body?
22. What is a pneumatic skeleton? What animals share this feature?
23. What is the function of a bird's air-sac system?
24. Name three bones in the skeleton of a sauropod and describe how they differ from the same three bones in a theropod like a chicken.
25. What is the function of the large bony crest (the deltopectoral crest) on the humerus of a bird?
26. Why do elephants walk on tiptoe?
27. Why were there caps of cartilage (gristle) at the end of the leg bones of the chickens you used?
28. How do paleontologists treat fossil bone to make it stronger?
29. Why is it incorrect to say that bones are turned into stone during fossilization?
30. What are the main differences between fossil bone and modern bone?
31. Can you tell the difference between fossil bone and modern bone by looking at them under the microscope?
32. Why should the plaster used to replace missing pieces of fossil bone be colored differently from the rest of the bone?
33. Why do the ribs of a dinosaur skeleton usually look so crooked?

34. How do animals get their scientific names?
35. What is a holotype?
36. Why is the name *Brontosaurus* no longer used by paleontologists?
37. What is a herbivore?
38. How do modern herbivores grind up their food?
39. How do paleontologists think sauropods ground up plants when most of them had such slender teeth?
40. Why do many birds peck up stones and swallow them?
41. What are some of the ways in which elephants reduce the impact of the stresses acting on their bones?
42. Why don't elephants lay down long to sleep?
43. Do giraffes have the same number of neck vertebrae as humans?
44. Why do elephants have a trunk?
45. What are some of the problems that giraffes have because of their long necks?
46. Explain how the blood circulates around the body, naming the vessels through which it flows.
47. Why do soldiers sometimes faint?
48. What evidence is there that sauropods lived on land, rather than in the water as was once believed?
49. What are ligaments?
50. What is the nuchal ligament, and how does it work?

# GLOSSARY

**Alula:** The small, winglike projection from the leading edge of a bird's wing, the equivalent of the bird's thumb.

**Anterior:** Toward the front, as opposed to posterior.

**Arteriole:** A small artery.

**Artery:** A blood vessel that carries blood away from the heart. Arteries have relatively thick walls compared with those of veins, and retain their shape even when empty of blood.

**Axis vertebra:** The second cervical (neck) vertebra. In birds, the axis vertebra has a laterally compressed centrum, i.e., the centrum is flattened from side to side.

**Bipedal:** An animal that moves on two legs. We are bipedal; so are kangaroos and birds.

**Capillary:** The smallest of blood vessels. The walls of capillaries are only one cell thick.

**Caudal vertebra:** A vertebra of the tail.

**Center of mass:** That point in a body through which gravity acts—the balance point of a body.

**Centrum:** The main part, or body, of a vertebra. Adjacent vertebrae articulate together by their centra, which are held together by intervertebral discs.

**Cervical:** Pertaining to the neck, as in the cervical vertebrae.

**Chevrons:** In reptiles, the Y-shaped bones that articulate with the posterior edges of the ventral surfaces of caudal vertebrae.

**Condyle:** The rounded process at the end of a bone that articulates with another bone.

**Coracoid:** The most ventral of the two bones forming the pectoral girdle. In reptiles, the coracoid tends to be rounded.

**Deltopectoral crest:** The bony crest that projects anteriorly from the lateral edge of the humerus. It is to the deltopectoral crest that the main flight muscles of birds attach.

**Dorsal:** Toward the back, as opposed to ventral. Our vertebral column is dorsal in position.

**Dorsal vertebrae:** Of reptiles, the vertebrae that lie between the pectoral girdle and sacrum. In birds and mammals these are referred to as thoracic vertebrae.

**Femur:** The upper bone of the hind leg, the thigh bone.

**Fibula:** The more slender of the two bones of the lower part of the hind leg. The fibula runs along the outside of the tibia (shin bone).

**Furcula:** The wishbone. Found in most living birds and in many theropod dinosaurs.

**Glycogen body:** A structure of uncertain function, found in the spinal region of living birds.

**Head of the femur:** The rounded process at the upper end of the femur that articulates with the hip socket.

**Herbivorous:** Plant-eating. Cows are herbivorous animals.

**Heterocoelic:** The term used to describe the saddle-shaped centra of birds.

**Humerus:** The upper bone of the foreleg.

**Hypapophysis:** A small bony protuberance from the ventral surface of the centrum in some vertebrae.

**Ilium:** The most dorsal of the three bones forming the pelvic girdle. The ilium articulates with the sacrum.

**Ischium:** The most posterior of the two bones of the pelvic girdle that lie ventral to the ilium.

**Keel** (of the sternum of birds): The ventral sheet of bone to which the main flight muscles attach.

**Lateral:** Toward the side of the body. Our arms are lateral to our ribs.

**Ligament:** The tough white sinew that connects one bone to another. Tendons are similar, but they attach muscles to bones.

**Major metacarpal:** The term used in the text for the largest of the two metacarpals of a bird (referred to informally as the hand bone). These two bones eventually fuse together as the skeleton matures, forming the terminal segment of the wing skeleton.

**Medial:** Toward the middle. Our ribs lie medial to our arms. *Median* has the same meaning.

**Metacarpal:** Part of the forelimb skeleton, equivalent to the palm of the hand.

**Metatarsal:** Part of the hind limb skeleton, equivalent to the sole of the foot.

**Nares:** The nostrils.

**Neural arch:** That portion of the vertebra that forms the neural canal, through which the spinal cord passes.

**Neural canal:** The canal formed by the neural arch, for passage of the spinal cord.

**Neural spine:** The medial process that extends dorsally from the neural arch of a vertebra. The neural spines are especially prominent in the dorsal vertebrae.

**Nuchal ligament:** The resilient (rubbery) ligament that runs along the dorsal aspect of the neck and which attaches to the back of the skull. Functions to help raise the lowered head.

**Orbit:** The bony eye socket in the skull.

**Ornithischia:** A major subdivision of the dinosaurs, characterized by a four-pronged pelvis. Ornithischian dinosaurs include the hadrosaurs, stegosaurs, horned dinosaurs, and ankylosaurs.

**Ossify:** To become converted into bone.

**Pectoral girdle:** The shoulder girdle.

**Pelvic girdle:** The pelvis.

**Pneumatic:** With reference to skeletons, this pertains to bones that are air-filled, as in many of the bones in the skeleton of a modern bird.

**Pneumatic foramen:** An aperture leading into the air-filled space inside a pneumatic bone. The humerus of the chicken has a well-developed pneumatic foramen.

**Posterior:** Toward the back, as opposed to anterior. A dog's tail is posterior in position.

**Pubis:** The most anterior of the two bones of the pelvic girdle that lie ventral to the ilium.

**Quadrupedal:** An animal that moves on four legs. A horse is quadrupedal.

**Radius:** The innermost bone of the forearm. Lies at the root of the thumb and is medial to the other forearm bone, the ulna.

**Respiratory:** Pertaining to breathing. The lungs are part of the respiratory system.

**Sacrum:** A series of vertebrae that are fused together to form an anchorage for the pelvic girdle.

**Saurischia:** A major subdivision of the dinosaurs, characterized by a three-pronged pelvis and comprising the theropods and sauropods.

**Sauropod:** One of the two groups of Saurischian dinosaurs. Sauropods are characterized by their large bodies, solid, robust limb bones, relatively small skulls, long necks and tails, and dorsally placed nares. *Apatosaurus* is a sauropod.

**Scapula:** The most dorsal of the two bones forming the pectoral girdle. The scapula is bladelike and is attached to the underlying ribs by muscles.

**Spinal cord:** Part of the central nervous system, the large nerve cord that runs along the back, from the brain to the end of the vertebral column.

**Sternal bone:** An informal term used in the text for a spade-shaped bone in a developing bird that eventually fuses with the rest of the sternum.

**Sternal rib:** The most ventral rib, which lies between the vertebral rib and the sternum.

**Sternum:** The median ventral bone to which the rib cage attaches. The sternum is well developed in birds, especially those that fly.

**Tendon:** The tough white sinew that connects a muscle to a bone. Ligaments are similar, but they attach bones together.

**Tetrapod:** Having four limbs. Birds, like humans, are bipedal tetrapods.

**Theropod:** One of the two groups of Saurischian dinosaurs. Theropods are characterized by having three fingers (usually), all ending in claws; three long metatarsal bones, tightly pressed together, which are often fused (joined); three main toes and a short big toe, all ending in claws; a femur that is slightly bowed forward; a fibula that is closely pressed against the tibia; and thin-walled, hollow limb bones.

**Thoracic:** Of birds and mammals, that part of the body that lies between the pectoral and sacral regions.

**Tibia:** The major bone of the lower hind leg—the shin bone.

**Transverse processes:** The paired lateral processes that extend from the base of the neural arch, on either side of a thoracic or dorsal vertebra, which articulate with a pair of ribs.

**Ulna:** The outermost bone of the forearm. Lies lateral to the other forearm bone, the radius.

**Uncinate process:** The bony projection from the posterior edge of a bird's rib that overlaps with the rib behind it, adding to the rigidity of the rib cage.

**Vein:** A blood vessel that returns blood to the heart. Veins have relatively thin walls compared with arteries, and collapse when not filled with blood. They also possess valves to ensure that the blood travels only in the direction of the heart.

**Ventral:** Toward the front or lower surface, as opposed to dorsal. Our sternum is ventral in position.

**Venule:** A small vein.

**Vertebral rib:** The true rib, which articulates with a vertebra, dorsally, and with a sternal rib, or the sternum, ventrally. Vertebral ribs are usually forked.

**Zygapophyses:** The paired processes extending from the anterior and posterior regions of the neural arch of a vertebra which articulate with those of the adjacent vertebrae. The articular surface of each anterior zygapophysis faces up and in, while that of a posterior zygapophysis faces down and out.

# FURTHER READING

Alexander, R. McN. 1985. Mechanics of posture and gait of some large dinosaurs. *Zoological Journal of the Linnaean Society* 83:1–25.

———. 1989. *Dynamics of dinosaurs and other extinct giants.* New York: Columbia University Press.

Bakker, R. T. 1978. Dinosaur feeding behavior and the origin of flowering plants. *Nature* 274:661–63.

Benton, M. J. 1990. Origin and interrelationships of dinosaurs. In *The Dinosauria*, ed. D. B. Weishampel, P. Dodson, and H. Osmólska. Berkeley: University of California Press. 11–30.

Berman, D. S., and J. S. McIntosh. 1978. Skull and relationships of the Upper Jurassic sauropod *Apatosaurus* (Reptilia, Saurischia). *Bulletin of Carnegie Museum of Natural History* 8:1–35.

Bird, R. T. 1944. Did *Brontosaurus* ever walk on land? *Natural History* 53:60–67.

Browne, M. W. 1996. Feathery fossil hints dinosaur-bird link. *New York Times*, October 19.

Bryant, H. N., and A. P. Russell. 1993. The occurrence of clavicles within the Dinosauria: Implications for the homology of the avian furcula and the utility of negative evidence. *Journal of Vertebrate Paleontology* 13:171–84.

Chatterjee, S. 1991. Cranial anatomy and relationships of a new Triassic bird from Texas. *Philosophical Transactions of the Royal Society of London, B* 332:277–342.

Chiappe, L. M. 1995. The first 85 million years of avian evolution. *Nature* 378:349–55.

Chure, D. J., and J. H. Madsen. 1996. The furcula in allosaurid theropods and its implication for determining bird origins. *Journal of Vertebrate Paleontology* (Abstracts of Papers) 16:28A.

Colbert, E. H. 1962. The weights of dinosaurs. *American Museum Novitiates* 2076:1–16.

Coombs, W. P. 1975. Sauropod habits and habitats. *Palaeogeography, Palaeoclimatology, Palaeoecology* 17:1–33.

———. 1978. Theoretical aspects of cursorial adaptions in dinosaurs. *Quarterly Review of Biology* 53:393–418.

Dodson, P. 1990. Sauropod paleoecology. In *The Dinosauria*, ed. D. B. Weishampel, P. Dodson, and H. Osmólska. Berkeley: University of California Press. 402–7.

Forster, C. A., L. M. Chiappe, D. W. Krause, and S. D. Sampson. 1996. The first Mesozoic avifauna from eastern Gondwana. *Journal of Vertebrate Paleontology* (Abstracts of Papers) 16:34A.

Garland, T. 1983. The relation between maximal running speed and body mass in terrestrial mammals. *Journal of Zoology, London* 199:157–70.

Gould, S. J. 1991. *Bully for Brontosaurus*. New York: Norton.

Hargens, A. R., R. W. Millard, K. Pettersson, and K. Johansen. 1978. Gravitational haemodynamics and oedema prevention in the giraffe. *Nature* 329:59–60.

Hohnke, L. A. 1973. Haemodynamics in the Sauropoda. *Nature* 244:309–10.

Horner, J. R., and D. B. Weishampel. 1988. A comparative embryological study of two ornithischian dinosaurs. *Nature* 332:256–57.

Ji, Q. and S. Ji. 1996. On the discovery of the earliest bird fossil in China and the origin of birds. *Chinese Geology*, 10: 30–33. [In Chinese].

Makovicky, P. J., and P. J. Currie. 1996. Discovery of a furcula in tyrannosaurid theropods. *Journal of Vertebrate Paleontology* (Abstracts of Papers) 16:34A.

Marsh, O. C. 1877. Notice of new dinosaurian reptiles from the Jurassic formations. *American Journal of Science* 14:514–16.

———. 1879. Notice of new Jurassic reptiles. *American Journal of Science* 18:501–5.

———. 1881. Principal characters of American Jurassic dinosaurs, Part V. *American Journal of Science* 21:417–23.

———. 1881. Principal characteristics of American Jurassic dinosaurs, Part VI. *American Journal of Science* 26:81–85.

Martin, J. 1987. Mobility and feeding in *Cetiosaurus* (Saurischia, Sauropoda)—Why the long neck? In *Fourth symposium on Mesozoic ecosystems,* ed. P. J. Currie and E. H. Koster. Drumheller, Canada: Tyrell Museum of Palaeontology. 150–55.

McGowan, C. 1991. *Dinosaurs, spitfires, and sea dragons.* Cambridge, Mass.: Harvard University Press.

———. 1994. *Diatoms to dinosaurs: the size and scale of living things.* Washington, D.C.: Island Press.

McIntosh, J. S. 1990. Sauropoda. In *The Dinosauria,* ed. D. B. Weishampel, P. Dodson, and H. Osmólska. Berkeley: University of California Press. 345–401.

McIntosh, J. S., and D. S. Berman. 1975. Description of the palate and lower jaw of the sauropod dinosaur *Diplodocus* (Reptilia: Saurischia) with remarks on the nature of the skull of *Apatosaurus. Journal of Paleontology* 49:187–99.

Norman, D. 1985. *The illustrated encyclopedia of dinosaurs.* London: Salamander.

Riggs, E. S. 1903. Structure and relationships of opisthocoelian dinosaurs. Part I, *Apatosaurus* Marsh. Field Columbian Museum, Geology Series Publication 82, 2:165–95.

Seymour, R. S. 1976. Dinosaurs, endothermy and blood pressure. *Nature* 262:207–8.

Warren, J. V. 1974. The physiology of the giraffe. *Scientific American* 231:96–105.

# INDEX